Praise for *Conversations with Terrorists*

"*Conversations with Terrorists* takes us inside t̶ labeled as enemies by successive U.S. governments. Rather than relying on State Department or Pentagon sources, Erlich interviews key Middle East players and presents their unvarnished views. Some have acted despicably; none of them are described as 'terrorists' by U.S. officials. A must read for anyone who wants to understand the phony War on Terror."

> —**Daniel Ellsberg**, *Secrets: A Memoir of Vietnam and the Pentagon Papers*

"Since I was present at two of these conversations with terrorists, I feel fully qualified to tell you that book you're holding is true, accurate, thoughtful, and eminently readable. I would expect no less of a man who would walk up to Khalil Meschal, the head of Hamas, at a Syrian embassy reception and ask for an interview. He got it. I traveled with Reese from the Souks of Damascus to the killing grounds of Al Sukariya near Iraq, where we investigated a secret U.S. raid together. It was like traveling with a pit-bull who is trailing a truck of raw meat. Reese locks on to an objective and will not be deterred until he has unpacked and deconstructed it from at least seven angles."

> —**Peter Coyote**, *Sleeping Where I Fall*

"In an era when the Bush Administration has defined the world as good vs. evil, it's great to read a book that reminds you things aren't all black and white, but rather shades of grey. *Conversations with Terrorists* shows you that the term *terrorist* is subjective and that one man's freedom fighter is another man's terrorist."

> —**Maz Jobrani**, comedian/actor/American citizen

"One of the most courageous journalists I know."

> —**Amiri Baraka** (aka **LeRoi Jones**), poet/playwright/political activist

"What is terror? A word. What is in that word *terror*? Reese Erlich introduces us to people whose names are associated with that word. He gives them the chance to speak. When we listen, we find ourselves provoked by unexpected insights and challenges to our stereotypes."

> —**Stephen Kinzer**, *All the Shah's Men*

"Reese Erlich is an investigative reporter par excellence: fearless, dogged, and someone who can't be snowed. Plus, he's a great writer."

> —**Matthew Rothschild**, editor, *The Progressive*

CONVERSATIONS WITH
TERRORISTS

Also by Reese Erlich

Target Iraq:
What the News Media Didn't Tell You
(co-authored with Norman Solomon)

The Iran Agenda:
The Real Story of U.S. Policy and the Middle East Crisis

Dateline Havana:
The Real Story of U.S. Policy and the Future of Cuba

CONVERSATIONS WITH
TERRORISTS

Middle East Leaders on
Politics, Violence, and Empire

REESE ERLICH

Foreword by
ROBERT BAER

Afterword by
NOAM CHOMSKY

PoliPointPress

Conversations with Terrorists: Middle East Leaders on Politics, Violence, and Empire

Copyright © 2010 by Reese Erlich

14   13   12   11   10   1   2   3   4   5

Portions of this book have appeared in different forms: "The Murders at al-Sukariya," co-authored with Peter Coyote, *Vanity Fair* online, Oct. 22, 2009; "On the Poppy Trail," *The Progressive*, November, 2009; "It's Not a Twitter Revolution in Iran," Reuters wire, June 26, 2009; "U.S. Aid Often Misses Targets in Afghanistan," *San Francisco Chronicle*, Oct. 4, 2009.

Production management: BookMatters
Book design: BookMatters
Cover design: Gerilyn Attebery

LIBRARY OF CONGRESS
CATALOGING-IN-PUBLICATION DATA

Erlich, Reese W., 1947–
  Conversations with terrorists : Middle East leaders on politics, violence, and empire / Reese Erlich.
    p. cm.
    Includes bibliographical references and index.
    ISBN 978-0-9824171-3-3 (alk. paper)
    1. Terrorism—Middle East. 2. War on Terrorism, 2001–2009. 3. United States—Foreign relations—Middle East. 4. Middle East—Foreign relations—United States. 5. Middle East—Politics and government—21st century. I. Title.
    HV6433.M5E75   2010
    363.3250956—dc22   2010018238

Published by:
PoliPointPress, LLC
80 Liberty Ship Way, Suite 22
Sausalito, CA 94965
(415) 339-4100
www.p3books.com

Distributed by Ingram Publisher Services
Printed in the USA

Contents

Foreword:
An Ex-CIA Perspective

I served as a field officer in the CIA from 1976 to 1997, experiencing firsthand many of the incidents described in *Conversations with Terrorists*. Erlich tells the personal stories of both well- and little-known Middle East players, weaving together a fascinating mosaic of how U.S. officials and media have misled the American people about the Middle East. He makes valuable suggestions on how to change U.S. policy and undermine extremists in the region.

I joined the CIA out of curiosity about other peoples and cultures. I first served in India, quickly moved to the Arab world, and was stationed in Lebanon during a very tumultuous time. I was particularly interested in the April 18, 1983, bombing of the U.S. Embassy in Beirut. It was a very good operation from a technical standpoint. The car bomber drove into the lobby, obstructed the guards' line of fire, and detonated the explosives—killing over 60 staff, CIA, and military personnel. We never did identify the driver; the truck was stolen and not traceable. On October 23, 1983, a similar truck bomb attack killed 299 American Marines and French soldiers in Beirut.

The U.S. government still blames Hezbollah for both bombings, part of the rationale for declaring it a terrorist organization today. As someone who personally investigated at the time, however, I can tell you that we still don't know who was responsible for the two bombings. We do know that the perpetrators were sophisticated militants attempting to drive the United States out of Lebanon.

Nevertheless, the Reagan White House and other American leaders denounced both bombings as unspeakable acts of terror. But it's just dumb to call the bombings "terrorism." Many Lebanese looked at the United States as colonizers. The Lebanese were waging a war of national liberation to get the foreigners out of their country. Lebanon had been a formal French colony until 1943; the United States landed Marines in Lebanon in 1958. Our presence in 1983 became a rallying cry for Shiites and other Lebanese opposed to foreign occupation. The attackers used bombs to kill foreign diplomats, soldiers, and intelligence officers. They were horrific, violent attacks, but they weren't acts of terrorism.

For its part, the U.S. government employed terrorist tactics to go after perceived enemies. In *Conversations with Terrorists*, Erlich provides valuable background about the ongoing turmoil in Lebanon. He describes how the CIA paid Saudi Arabians to assassinate Ayatollah Mohammad Fadlallah. The CIA was convinced Fadlallah had masterminded the Marine barracks bombing. The Saudis hired Lebanese operatives to plant a powerful car bomb outside Fadlallah's apartment building. He wasn't injured, but the bomb murdered 80 people and wounded 200.

The CIA had the wrong guy. Fadlallah was politically independent of Hezbollah and opposed Iranian influence in Lebanon. Today Fadlallah is a respected Grand Ayatollah seeking reconciliation among the various political factions. There have been far too many similar cases in the so-called Global War on Terrorism.

Today Hezbollah is a very different organization than it was in the 1980s. Its members aren't trying to convert Christians to Islam. Even Christian and Sunni Muslim leaders concede that Hezbollah is an important parliamentary force. Christians form political alliances with Hezbollah and run as partners in its political coalition. In a very real sense, Hezbollah helps keep a lid on Lebanon's fractious and sometimes violent politics. Hezbollah stopped firing rockets across the Israeli border and, while it will fight if attacked, has no intention of starting a war with that country. Hezbollah has grown up.

The Palestinian group Hamas has changed as well. In the early 1990s, it carried out a series of horrific suicide bombings inside Israel and the occupied territories. Yahya Abd-al-Latif Ayyash, known as "the Engineer," became famous for terrorizing Israelis. He was responsible for the deaths of an estimated 90 people; Hamas killed a total of over 500 Israelis during the campaign. In 1996 Israel's Shin Bet intelligence agency assassinated Ayyash with a cell phone rigged with explosives.

By 2005 Hamas changed course and stopped all suicide bombings. Israelis are relatively safer today, not because of the wall they built between Israel and parts of Palestine, but because Hamas made a conscious decision to end suicide attacks.

In January 2006, Hamas won free and fair parliamentary elections in the Palestinian Authority. Hamas leadership indicated they were ready to make significant political changes, but the United States and Israel instead sought to attack and isolate the group. The United States should see if Hamas is serious about allowing implementation of UN Resolution 242, which calls for returning all Arab land and the creation of two states in exchange for peace. Simply calling Hamas "terrorists" does nothing to advance the peace process.

Conversations with Terrorists does an excellent job of showing that the definition of "terrorist" depends on who is throwing the bomb. Erlich writes about the Stern Gang and Irgun, two Zionist groups that used terrorist tactics against the British and Arabs in the 1940s. The Irgun blew up Jerusalem's King David Hotel in 1946, killing 90 Jews, Arabs, and British officials. The world has largely forgotten the incident. Leaders of those terrorist groups, Menachem Begin and Yitzhak Shamir, later went on to become prime ministers of Israel.

In more recent times, the United States has been happy to ally with groups using terrorist tactics. In the 1980s, the United States embraced the right-wing Christian Lebanese Forces, whose members massacred civilians in Beirut's Palestinian refugee camps. That same militia kidnapped four Iranian diplomats and executed them. We have a habit of not looking too closely at the actions of our allies, but in the end, we get held responsible for their actions.

U.S. credibility around the world is similarly undermined by the use of torture and detention without trial. How can we claim to uphold the rule of law when we torture suspects, often innocent civilians, in places like Baghdad's Abu Ghraib, Bagram base in Afghanistan, and Guantanamo? The U.S. reputation certainly suffered by supporting the Contras in Nicaragua and other human rights violators in Central America, but the Bush years made things even worse. Today, what separates the U.S. policy from that of authoritarian regimes in the Middle East?

The American firebombing of Germany in 1945 was terrorism. We didn't focus on military or industrial targets. We wanted to terrify the civilian population so the German military would surrender. That's what al Qaeda wants to do on a smaller scale today. That was the intention of 9/11. But al Qaeda has no chance of success and has created the opposite effect. The 9/11 attacks rallied support for America around the world while alienating most of the Muslim population. There was a huge wave of Muslim revulsion. Most Muslims find bin Laden repulsive.

By invading and occupying Afghanistan and Iraq, and carrying out another war in Pakistan, however, the United States has actually helped recruit extremists. The United States tries to link al Qaeda to every Muslim group opposed to U.S. policy, but it's a conscious lie.

The CIA agents and analysts I know are much more intelligent than the propaganda fed to the public. They don't throw around the term "terrorism." Terrorism is a tactic; it's not a strategy. We understood that. When the CIA chief of station in Lebanon was kidnapped, it wasn't an end in itself. It was a tactic to get the United States out of Lebanon. We understood the differences between militant Sunni and Shia groups, and between the various governments of the Middle East. We never lumped them all together as terrorists.

But the CIA leadership with offices on the seventh floor of CIA headquarters goes along with White House policy. They are selling war to the American people. So they repeat the lie that the Muslims are coming to get us. If we don't stop them on the Kabul River, they'll be pulling up to the Delaware River.

Unfortunately, President Barack Obama is continuing these same, wrong policies. He's a prisoner of the U.S. military. Obama can't take on the generals. They may ask for 75,000 more troops for Afghanistan. He can't afford to tell the military that's enough, because he can't risk someone like General David Petraeus resigning. The last thing you need is an unhappy general when fighting tough battles on health care or similar domestic issues. The U.S. military didn't originally like going into Afghanistan, but once there, they want to make it look like they've won.

Continued troop escalations in Afghanistan won't win the war. We've got to get our troops out. Foreign troops in a country only succeed in rallying people against the occupier. We've got to undermine the jihadists politically. Individual countries must fight the battle against their own extremists. The jihadist movement collapsed in Saudi Arabia, for example, because people became repulsed with their violence against fellow Muslims.

Conversations with Terrorists offers many insights into the phony War on Terrorism. Today most Americans oppose the wars in Iraq and Afghanistan. They don't trust Washington, the wars cost too much, and too many American troops are dying. But the American people don't necessarily understand the situation on the ground in those countries or the extent of the lying in Washington. *Conversations with Terrorists* provides that important background.

Robert Baer
Beirut
March 28, 2010

Former CIA field officer Robert Baer authored the book *See No Evil,* which later became the film *Syriana.*

one

Will the Real Terrorists Please Stand Up?

AS I WALK DOWN THE STREET in Belfast, Northern Ireland, one day in 1985, British soldiers in armored vehicles point their assault rifles directly at my head. It isn't personal. They do that to every pedestrian. I am in Belfast to write a story about the Irish Republican Army (IRA), long vilified as terrorists by the U.S. and British governments.

That's where I meet Liam, a decommissioned member of the IRA. Decommissioned means that he was at one time an active-duty guerrilla, but after his release from prison he joined Sinn Fein, the legal political party fighting to reunite the two parts of Ireland. They are not fighting a religious war between Protestants and Catholics, he explains. It's a political battle between republicans, who demand reunification, and unionists, who want the north to remain part of Britain.

Liam had just served seven hard years in a British prison for shooting at British soldiers stationed in Belfast. "Why were you locked up?" I ask. "I missed," he says with a devilish smile. Aha—a real terrorist in the flesh.

One night he offers to take me for drinks at the "feelin" club, which I initially think is some kind of Irish republican topless bar. The club stands surrounded by large boulders placed some distance away from the building's stone walls, which prevent cars packed with explosives from parking too close. Nothing like a little plastique to ruin your Guinness.

When we arrive at the club, a man asks if I am a "feelin?" Noting my puzzled look, he explains in his heavy Irish brogue that a "feelin" is someone convicted of a serious crime, much worse than a misdemeanor. Only republicans convicted of felonies are allowed into the club. The place is packed.

I was arrested for felony conspiracy for organizing a large anti–Vietnam War demonstration in 1967. (I don't mention my acquittal.) "That'll do," he says, stamping my hand and showing me in the front door. Over numerous pints of Guinness, Liam and I talk about politics and violence. I have one key question. Why does the IRA bomb innocent civilians as well as military targets?

Liam, conceding that the IRA sometimes uses terrorist tactics, explains a debate within the group. Some argue that they should attack only soldiers and British officials in order to sway Irish and British public opinion against colonial rule. Hard-liners, on the other hand, favor bombing civilian targets in London and other cities to show that the occupation is untenable. Yes, we alienate British public opinion, they admit, but the population will become so fed up with the violence that they will finally give in to IRA demands.

I express sharp disagreement with the hard-line view. Alienating so many potential allies is not only immoral but politically counterproductive. Precisely that debate would continue for many years within the IRA. At times the group stopped killing civilians, and at times the bombings resumed. Ultimately, the IRA gave up armed struggle in return for British guarantees of power-sharing and an end to discrimination against Catholics and the republican community.

My conversations with Liam have stayed with me all these years. The IRA was not a terrorist organization, although it certainly used terrorist tactics at times. The anti-Nazi resistance in Europe used assassinations and bombings, but no one today calls them terrorists. That's important to remember when analyzing groups in the Middle East. After all, the U.S. government itself has used terrorist tactics numerous times to overthrow legitimate governments. So who is the real terrorist? Does the term even have any meaning in today's world? Sixteen years after my visit to Belfast, I was about to find out.

I AM AWAKENED by an agitated caller on the morning of September 11, 2001. A producer friend traveling on the East Coast calls to tell me to turn on the TV. I see the footage of the planes smashing into the World Trade Center, and the chaos engulfing the Pentagon and downtown Manhattan. The images of people running down the street followed by billowing clouds of smoke are singed in my memory. Like millions of others around the world, I sit transfixed, trying to make sense of the events. The world is outraged. Even the American government's most ardent enemies—from militant Palestinian groups, to Muslim clerics in Lebanon and even the Taliban in Afghanistan—express sympathy with the victims of a senseless terrorist attack.[1]

Months later, I am on assignment, interviewing Muslim Chechen refugees forced out of their province in Russia. When they learn I am American, their first words are of sympathy for the victims of 9/11. Here are people living in tents in a hostile part of the world, completely dependent on international aid for survival, and expressing solidarity with America. Soon, however, U.S. government actions managed to transform this outpouring of international sympathy into unparalleled hatred, all because of what the Bush administration reduced to an ominous acronym: GWOT, the Global War on Terrorism.

The Bush administration claimed terrorists were everywhere. Terrorists were planning to explode nuclear dirty bombs in major cities. Saddam Hussein was instructing terrorists to bomb our seaports with suitcase atomic weapons. Bush would eventually lump together al Qaeda, Palestinians fighting for a homeland, Iraqis and Afghans fighting foreign occupation, Basque separatists, and Marxist guerrillas in Colombia. Arabs and Muslims became the new scapegoats. The American people were led to believe that terrorists had sleeper cells deep inside the country that were waiting for words of incitement from Muslim imams. Boarding a plane while Muslim became a quasi-criminal offense. Congress passed a resolution authorizing war in Afghanistan that President Bush interpreted as carte blanche to invade anywhere.[2] The Bush administration decided it had unlimited powers for domestic repression as well.

But the War on Terrorism never made sense. You can wage war against an enemy country or insurgency, but you can't wage war on a tactic. Real wars begin and end. How can you tell when you've won the War on Terror? Because the war might never end, military intervention abroad and repression at home could also continue indefinitely. Even after the resounding Republican defeat in the 2008 elections, and the disasters in Iraq and Afghanistan, former vice president Dick Cheney continued to defend the Global War on Terrorism as the basis for unlimited military intervention. "Up until 9/11, it [terrorism] was treated as a law enforcement problem. Once you go into a wartime situation . . . then you use all of your assets to go after the enemy. You go after the state sponsors of terror, places where they've got sanctuary."[3]

Those places of sanctuary, apparently, keep multiplying. On September 10, 2001, the United States was not engaged in combat anywhere in the world. Nine years later, the United States has occupied Afghanistan and Iraq, and it sends troops to fight "terrorists" in Pakistan, Yemen, and Somalia. U.S. drones fire missiles to attack targets in Pakistan, Iraq, Afghanistan, Yemen, and East

Africa. The American people, not to mention civilians around the world, are far less safe today than before the start of GWOT.

PART OF THE PROBLEM is how the United States defines terrorism. The State Department writes that terrorism is an activity that "(1) involves a violent act or an act dangerous to human life, property, or infrastructure; and (2) appears to be intended to intimidate or coerce a civilian population; to influence the policy of a government by intimidation or coercion; or to affect the conduct of a government by mass destruction, assassination, kidnapping, or hostage-taking."[4]

Not surprisingly, the U.S.-government definition of terrorism assumes that terrorists are those who attack established governments; it makes no mention of government use of terrorist tactics. I prefer a different formulation. I think terrorism is the intentional murder or injury of civilians, or the destruction of their property, for purposes of intimidating the population and effecting political change. Terrorism of that kind can be perpetrated by individuals, groups, or countries. In addition, any definition of terrorism should consider whether the action takes place in the context of a war, including wars of national liberation. Terrorism would then include both the 9/11 attacks on the World Trade Center buildings and Israeli Defense Forces dropping 500-pound bombs on apartment buildings to allegedly kill one Hamas leader. The simple act of setting off a car bomb against enemy troops or assassinating enemy officers is not, by itself, terrorism.

From a practical perspective, however, the United States has rendered the term "terrorism" meaningless. Pro–United States insurgents who bomb innocent civilians are called freedom fighters. In the 1980s, such heroes included the U.S.-backed Afghan mujahedeen fighting the Soviet occupation and the U.S.-trained

Contras fighting the Sandinistas in Nicaragua. On the other hand, every guerrilla using violence to oppose the United States and its allies is automatically labeled a terrorist. Even nonviolent opponents of the United States offering political and economic aid to alleged insurgents are defined as terrorist supporters. The United States government has shut down Islamic charities sending donations to schools in Palestine because of alleged connections to Hamas. The hypocrisy list is endless.

Students of recent American history shouldn't be surprised. Although claiming to be staunch opponents of terrorism, the United States and its allies frequently use terrorist tactics themselves.

IF YOU THINK of airplane piracy or car bombings, what image comes to mind? Most Americans picture a bearded Muslim extremist. The fact is, Lechi, a Zionist group also known as the Stern Gang, was the first to use letter bombs, thereby pioneering the use of terror tactics in the modern era. In 1947, when Britain controlled colonial Palestine, Stern Gang commander Yaakov Eliav orchestrated the mailing of letter bombs addressed to members of the British cabinet and other officials.[5] From 1945 to 1948, the Stern Gang and another right-wing Zionist group, the Irgun, engaged in kidnappings, assassinations, and car bombings against both British officials and Arab civilians. (For much more detail on early Zionist terrorists, see chapter 3.)

Several years later, in 1954, the Israeli government performed the first act of air piracy in the Middle East. Israeli planes forced a Syrian civilian plane to land in Israel in a vain effort to trade the passengers for Israeli agents captured in Syria. Israeli prime minister Moshe Sharett admitted that "our action was without precedent in the history of international practice."[6]

After World War II, the United States expanded its empire by seeking control of former European colonies around the world. But the United States didn't utilize the discredited system of colonies; it preferred to establish neo-colonies, formally independent countries that were actually under U.S. control. To consolidate power, the United States backed right-wing insurgents, monarchists, and militarists—often using terrorism to intimidate and confuse civilians. Below are some examples of those U.S. efforts.

The CIA instigated a destabilization campaign in French-controlled Vietnam in the early 1950s, backing militarists as a so-called third force opposed to both the French and the Communist Party. The CIA used terrorist tactics to intentionally kill civilians and sow confusion, as when a car bomb killed civilians in front of the Saigon Opera House in 1952.[7] The Graham Greene novel and recent film, *The Quiet American,* portrayed such incidents accurately.

In 1953, the CIA organized a coup against the democratically elected government of Iranian prime minister Mohammad Mossadegh. Iran had nationalized British petroleum. The United States and Britain wanted to maintain control over Iran's oil and establish military bases. In declassified documents, the CIA admits to carrying out assassinations and bombings to weaken Mossadegh and return the shah (king) to power.[8]

Beginning in 1961, the CIA organized a vicious campaign of arson, bombings, and assassinations against Cuba. The U. S. government trained Cuban exiles to burn cane fields, destroy crops and livestock, and attempt to assassinate Cuban leaders, including Fidel Castro. The 1975 U.S. Senate Church Commission documented many of these attacks.[9]

After the Sandinista revolution in Nicaragua, the Reagan administration created a counterrevolutionary militia, known as the Contras. The U.S. Army- and CIA-trained and funded Contras attacked soft targets, such as schools, health clinics, and agricultural cooperatives in order to weaken support for the Sandinistas. Contra leader Horacio Arce said, "We attack a lot of schools, health centers, and those sort of things. We have tried to make it so that the Nicaraguan government cannot provide social services for the peasants, cannot develop its project . . . that's the idea."[10]

In the 1980s the CIA funded, trained, and armed the mujahedeen, so-called freedom fighters, to oppose Soviet troops in Afghanistan. These right-wing fundamentalists intentionally targeted movie theaters, cultural events, and university professors, among others. Some of the mujahedeen who received this training were later arrested for terrorist attacks inside the United States. For example, Ramzi Yousef received training in Pakistan during this period and was later convicted for bombing the New York World Trade Center in 1993. Osama bin Laden himself was a major fundraiser for the mujahedeen and was based in Pakistan.

And lest you think that such terrorist tactics are ancient history, consider recent U.S. actions. Under presidents Clinton, Bush, and Obama, the United States has carried out "extraordinary renditions," in which suspected terrorists are kidnapped, indefinitely detained, and tortured in secret CIA prisons or those of allies. The workings of the program became embarrassingly public in the case of Muslim cleric Osama Mustafa Hassan Nasr. He disappeared in 2003, while walking to a mosque in Milan. The CIA, in cooperation with Italian intelligence, kidnapped Nasr, flew him from a U.S. military base in Italy to Germany, and eventually to Egypt, where he was brutally tortured. The United States accused him of membership in a fundamentalist group seeking to overthrow the Egyptian government. The Egyptians released him in 2007.

How do we know the CIA did it? Italian investigators pieced together the information from cell phone logs and luxury hotel receipts used by CIA operatives and their Italian counterparts.

In November 2009, an Italian judge convicted 22 CIA employees in abstentia. Italy issued arrest warrants. As of the writing of this book, the United States refuses to extradite them, and they remain free—although vacations in Italy are no longer an option.[11]

The U.S. government has never admitted the full extent of its terror operations. But it regularly exaggerates the terrorist danger from its enemies. The Global War on Terrorism is modeled directly on the anticommunist campaigns of years past, something I remember all too well.

IN 1964 I SKIPPED A DAY of high school to campaign for Lyndon Johnson and Hubert Humphrey. I thought Johnson was the peace candidate opposed to the warmonger Barry Goldwater. In reality, Johnson would continue escalating the war in Vietnam, just as Goldwater would have done. But in that era, the vast majority of Americans united behind our president to stop the spread of communism in Vietnam.

I believed the U.S. propaganda of the time. Vietnam was a tool of the Chinese communists. If Vietnam fell, so would all of Southeast Asia, according to what was called the "domino theory." Communists would then be in a stronger position to invade the United States and our allies in Asia and Western Europe. This mantra was an earlier version of the current "We're fighting them over there so we don't have to fight them here."

In reality, Vietnam posed no threat to the people of the United States, nor does it today. After the 1975 U.S. defeat in Indochina, Vietnam reunited as one country. Some pro-U.S. members of the armed forces and government officials were killed; others were sent to internment camps. Some ordinary civilians fled the country as boat people. But today the country is more prosperous than under U.S. rule, and the Vietnamese themselves are making economic reforms. The United States and Vietnam have normal diplomatic and trade relations. Even if you believe that the Vietnamese live under a totalitarian dictatorship and are therefore worse off than before 1975, Vietnam clearly poses no military threat to the United States.

U.S. policies have actually spread insurgency to other countries. Had the United States never invaded Vietnam, communist-led revolutions in Laos and Cambodia would probably not have succeeded. In fact, by overthrowing the popular Prince Sihanouk and installing a military dictator in Cambodia, the United States paved the way to victory for the horrific Khmer Rouge.[12] The war in Indochina killed over 58,000 American soldiers, some 3 million to 4 million Vietnamese on both sides, and 1.5 million to 2 million Cambodians and Laotians. As one Vietnam vet friend told me, "Remind me again why we fought that war?"

<hr/>

CONDITIONS TODAY ARE DIFFERENT than during the Vietnam era. But then, as now, the U.S. government intentionally exaggerates a threat to scare Americans and justify expansion of its empire. After the Soviet Union collapsed in 1991, the United States could no longer argue that it faced a danger of invasion from evil communists.[13] Many Americans envisioned a peace dividend, which could fund domestic programs once the United States closed military bases and cut defense spending. A funny thing happened on the way to collecting that dividend, however. It disappeared. From 1991 to 1999, the U.S. military did close some domestic military bases and somewhat reduced military spending. But starting with the U.S. invasion of Kosovo under President Clinton in 1999, the United States massively increased military spending once again. By 2008, the United States had allocated $616 billion for the military, more than twice what was spent in 1991.[14]

Today, the United States spends more on its military than any country in history, accounting for 48 percent of all military spending in the world.[15] It maintains some 737 military bases globally with 1.4 million active duty soldiers.[16] U.S. nuclear missiles, a huge naval fleet, and advanced jet fighters and bombers are particularly ill-suited to fight small groups of insurgents using terrorist tactics. But that's not the intention. The U.S. military protects and expands an imperialist empire.

In case you have trouble thinking of the United States in those terms, let me offer an analogy. We have no difficulty understanding that Britain had a large imperialist empire prior to World War II. The British elite benefited economically from its control of the natural resources of its colonies and neo-colonies. The British maintained huge military forces able to control their territories, ensure supplies of oil and coal, control sea lanes, and protect vital choke points, such as the Suez Canal. British leaders sought to deny competing imperialist powers control of vital resources and strategic military sites. The British installed friendly governments in third world countries and made sure those governments stayed in power.

Is the United States today any different? Let's examine the issue of oil. In 1980, President Jimmy Carter declared what became known as the "Carter Doctrine." Using the excuse of the Soviet invasion of Afghanistan, the doctrine asserts the U.S. right to control Middle East oil, using military force when necessary. The region, according to Carter, "contains more than two-thirds of the world's exportable oil. The Soviet effort to dominate Afghanistan has brought Soviet military forces to within 300 miles of the Indian Ocean and close to the Straits of Hormuz, a waterway through which most of the world's oil must flow. The Soviet Union is now attempting to consolidate a strategic position, therefore, that poses a grave threat to the free movement of Middle East oil."[17] The doctrine has remained U.S. policy to this day.

If U.S. policy was really just a response to the "Soviet threat," that policy would have changed as the Soviet Union collapsed.

However, U.S. aggression in the region increased. In 1990 the United States invaded Iraq in the first Gulf War, which returned oil-rich Kuwait to the pro-U.S. camp;[18] in 2001 the United States invaded and occupied Afghanistan; in 2003 the United States invaded and occupied Iraq. As a direct result of these policies, U.S. oil companies were able to reap record-breaking profits both from the Middle East and elsewhere.

The expansion of empire increases the number of Americans living in far-flung outposts who can be attacked by insurgents. If the Global War on Terrorism is going so well, why do we keep sending troops to more countries?

IN OCTOBER 1999, I reported from Pakistan just days after a military coup led by General Pervez Musharraf. I interviewed leaders of ultraconservative fundamentalist parties, who complained about crackdowns by the new government; at that time, they admitted they had almost no popular support. But after the U.S. invasion of Afghanistan two years later, those ultraconservative parties gradually became popular. Pakistanis became outraged at U.S. occupation policies that killed innocent civilians while supposedly targeting terrorists. A whole new organization emerged, the Pakistani Taliban. Today Pakistan is facing a virtual civil war as insurgents blow up both civilian and military targets.

The United States long tried to cover up its military role in Pakistan, but some reports leaked out. Blackwater (renamed Xe) mercenaries were helping to load and guide the drone missiles inside Pakistan. Then in February 2010, three American soldiers dressed as civilians were killed during an insurgent bombing. Subsequently, the U.S. government admitted that 200 U.S. soldiers were acting as "trainers" in Pakistan.[19] Simultaneously, the CIA organized dozens of raids inside Pakistan hunting for alleged terrorists.[20]

Extending GWOT to Pakistan has had a horrific impact. In 2009, 3,021 Pakistani civilians died due to suicide bombings and similar attacks, a 33 percent increase over the previous year. A 2009 report from the Pakistan Institute for Peace Studies, a nonprofit research group, counts a total of 12,632 war-related deaths, including 667 killed by U.S. drone attacks.[21] A Pew Global Attitudes opinion poll released in August 2009 indicated that 61 percent of Pakistanis had an unfavorable view of al Qaeda, whereas 64 percent saw the United States as the enemy.[22] Pakistanis want neither extremists nor the United States meddling in their country.

ON CHRISTMAS DAY 2009, Nigerian citizen Umar Farouk Abdulmutallab was arrested for allegedly trying to set off a bomb on a Detroit-bound flight. He reportedly told investigators he had received training from a Yemen-based al Qaeda group. That arrest spotlighted yet one more country targeted in the clandestine part of the war on terror. Yemen is one of the poorest countries in the Middle East and has a 40 percent unemployment rate. The United States contributed to this problem when it cut off all aid in 1991 because Yemen failed to back the first Gulf War. At the same time, U.S.-ally Saudi Arabia expelled 850,000 Yemeni workers from that country, causing a massive wave of unemployment from which it still hasn't recovered. The Yemen government exercises little control outside the capital city of Sana. The government is besieged by rebel groups in both the north and south, neither of which have ties to al Qaeda.

Amid all these troubles, or perhaps because of them, Yemen has become the second most heavily armed country in the world on a per capita basis. The country has enough AK-47s and rocket-propelled grenade launchers to provide arms to one-third of the population. In gun ownership, however, Yemen trails the United

States, where there are enough small weapons to arm 95 percent of the population.[23]

The Yemeni branch of al Qaeda, only loosely connected to Osama bin Laden, takes advantage of the instability in Yemen to spread its right-wing, fundamentalist message. Al Qaeda members from other countries reportedly have married into Yemeni clans to strengthen their local ties. The United States military and intelligence agencies have carried out drone attacks inside Yemen, angering many Yemenis and helping al Qaeda gain some sympathy. In 2002 U.S. drones killed several alleged al Qaeda members. In December 2009, U.S. intelligence and missiles were responsible for another attack that killed 49 civilians, including 23 children and 17 women.[24]

Yemen has small-scale oil production and ranks only 36th among the world's oil-producing countries, but empires have coveted the country for years. The Yemeni city of Aden sits astride the entrance to the Red Sea and thus controls access to the Suez Canal. According to former Indian diplomat M. K. Bhadrakumar, "Control of Aden and the Malacca Strait will put the U.S. in an unassailable position in the 'great game' of the Indian Ocean. The sea lanes of the Indian Ocean are literally the jugular veins of China's economy. By controlling them, Washington sends a strong message to Beijing that any notions by the latter that the U.S. is a declining power in Asia would be nothing more than an extravagant indulgence in fantasy."[25]

The British Empire sought economic and military control of the Middle East for the benefit of its ruling elite. How is the United States today any different?

THE UNITED STATES CONTINUES to repeat many of the same mistakes it made in Iraq and Afghanistan. Local religious extremists are happy to take advantage of U.S. actions to promote their own ideology. Anwar al-Awlaki is an American Muslim cleric whom the United States accuses of being affiliated with al Qaeda in Yemen. He, like other al Qaeda supporters, calls for the creation of an Islamic caliphate (religious empire) throughout the Middle East. In an Al Jazeera interview, he cleverly mixes popular criticisms of the United States with his own distorted version of Islam. He says that U.S. leaders "want to market the democratic and peaceful U.S. Islam that calls for obeying the superiors even if they were traitors and collaborators, they want an Islam that recognizes the occupation and deals with it, they want an Islam that has no Sharia ruling, no jihad and no Islamic caliphate."[26]

Asked if he supported blowing up the Detroit-bound airplane on Christmas, he says military targets are better, but killing civilians is legitimate because "the American people live [in] a democratic system and that is why they are held responsible for their policies. The American people are the ones who have voted twice for Bush the criminal and elected Obama, who is not different from Bush as his first remarks stated that he would not abandon Israel, despite the fact that there were other antiwar candidates in the U.S. elections, but they won very few votes. The American people take part in all its government's crimes." This ideological justification for killing innocent civilians reminds me of right-wing Americans who demand harsh treatment of all Palestinians because they voted for Hamas in democratic elections.

Luckily, al-Awlaki, Osama bin Laden, and al Qaeda have little support in the Middle East. Popular opinion turned sharply against fundamentalists in Iraq and Pakistan when they began blowing up Muslims in the name of Islam. But that's not the case for organizations such as Hamas and Hezbollah, which have armed militias but also function as legal political parties that poll significant votes in parliamentary elections. In that sense, they have more in common with the Irish Republican Army than with al Qaeda. And that's where my old friend Liam comes back into the story.

IT'S HARD TO IMAGINE many similarities between the Middle East today and 1985 Belfast, particularly given the popularity of Irish pub quizzes. One night Liam convinces me to participate in such a quiz. It's a game similar to Jeopardy in which two teams compete to answer trivia questions while interacting with Mr. Johnnie Walker. I become a local hero when I answer simple questions about Greek philosophy and Roman emperors. I fail the republican cause, however, when I am unable to say who won the soccer World Cup in 1933.

Liam continues my education in recent Irish history. The British engaged in a divide-and-rule strategy by giving power to Protestant leaders in Northern Ireland. In the 1950s and '60s, Catholics launched a nonviolent civil rights movement calling for an end to discrimination in housing and education, and for equal voting rights. The British government responded with brutal repression. The 1968 police beating of peaceful marchers in Derry attracted worldwide attention. The Provisional IRA was born out of this struggle and took up arms against the British. It considered itself a national liberation movement, as legitimate as all the other anti-colonial struggles of the era. Initially, the IRA targeted British security forces and officials, but civilians were inevitably killed as well.

The British army and unionist paramilitaries used even more violence against the republicans. The British established special kangaroo courts to try accused terrorists, systematically tortured prisoners, and armed unionist paramilitaries who used car bombs and assassinations to deadly effect. These right-wing paramilitaries made no pretense of targeting republican leaders; they killed Catholics indiscriminately. By the time of my 1985 visit, Liam didn't think the IRA could win militarily, but neither could the British crush them.

Over the next 20 years, the IRA put increasing emphasis on political organizing while continuing armed actions, including a devastating bombing in a London financial office building in 1996. In 1997 the IRA declared a ceasefire and a year later agreed to the Good Friday accords, in which it stopped armed struggle in return for the promised withdrawal of British troops, power-sharing in a new government, release of political prisoners, and an end to discrimination.

Sinn Fein became one of the top vote-getting parties in Northern Ireland and eventually shared power with a leading unionist party. The underlying issues of discrimination and colonial ties to Britain are not yet resolved, and the struggle continues through political means. U.S. leaders often use the example of the IRA as a potential model for disarming Middle East terrorist groups. That argument would be far more persuasive if the British had agreed to end colonial rule.

Nevertheless, we can draw some positive lessons from the IRA experience. A resistance group with legitimate demands and a popular base of support should be treated seriously, not vilified as terrorists. Both the dominant power and the resistance group have to make meaningful concessions. Once a political settlement is reached, the issue of armed violence becomes far less significant and eventually disappears.

Instead of labeling all opponents as terrorists, the United States should distinguish between different groups in the Middle East. The intractable right-wing leaders of groups such as al Qaeda should be arrested and tried. On the other hand, the United States should recognize the legitimate demands of national liberation movements, even those that use terrorist tactics. For a better understanding of what such groups stand for, let's start with my exclusive interview with Hamas leader Khaled Meshal.

KHALED MESHAL,
chair of Hamas Political Bureau

Photo credit: Wikicommons: Creative Commons Attribution 3.0; Trango

two

Hamas's Khaled Meshal: Middle East's Most Wanted

AT EXACTLY FOUR IN THE AFTERNOON, a taxi driver delivers us to a small sentry post manned by an armed soldier on a quiet, residential street in Damascus. The Palestinian group Hamas operates its head-quarters-in-exile here under Syrian protection. I'm here to interview Khaled Meshal, the top Hamas leader. In 1997, while Meshal was living in Jordan, Israeli Mossad agents poisoned him in an unsuc-cessful assassination attempt. Needless to say, security is tight. Two men in civilian clothes carrying AK-47 assault rifles arrive at a trot and lead us into a small foyer. I'm traveling with actor and writer Peter Coyote on his first trip to the Middle East. It was to be quite a baptism, particularly because we're both Jewish.

Inside the Hamas office, four more security men surround us in silence and begin to go over our clothing in a way that makes U.S. airport screenings seem like a Montessori school exercise. They con-fiscate our cell phones, finger the seams of our jeans and shirts by the inch, turn pockets inside out, dismantle a fountain pen, and run their fingers around the tops of socks and inside the waistband of our pants. These guys are focused, sharp, and extremely disciplined. We were to wait hours for our interview, which would offer new insights into the Israeli-Palestinian conflict and the wider issue of terrorism. But first some background on Hamas.

HAMAS IS ONE OF THE MOST FEARED and misunderstood groups in the Middle East. Although it began as a Muslim fundamentalist group opposed to the existence of Israel, Israeli authorities initially supported it as an alternative to the Palestine Liberation Organization (PLO). Hamas was the first group to use suicide bombers in the Israeli-Palestinian conflict, killing over 500 Israelis in the early 1990s. More recently, it has killed civilians by launching homemade rockets into Israeli towns.

Hamas spends most of its budget on education, medical care, and other social services for impoverished Palestinians. It won free and fair parliamentary elections in 2006, and enjoys substantial popular support throughout the Middle East. For many Palestinians, Hamas is a resistance group fighting Israeli occupation. For Israelis, Americans, and other Westerners, Hamas is synonymous with terrorism. In many ways Hamas resembles the nationalist and fundamentalist Jewish groups that fought British occupation before Israel's independence in 1948, although neither would appreciate the comparison. At that time, right-wing Jewish zealots used terrorist tactics against the British and the Arabs, always citing Jewish nationalism and the Bible as justification. Hamas uses a strict—and false—reading of the Koran to make no distinction between Israeli soldiers and civilians. After the end of British rule, the Jewish terrorists became a legitimate part of the Israeli political system.[1] Will Hamas be any different?

One thing is for sure: Israeli and Western governments consciously distort Hamas's political views. For example, Western governments and media regularly claim that Hamas seeks the destruction of Israel and wouldn't be satisfied with an independent Palestinian state next to Israel. But in our interview, Meshal says that Israel rejects this two-state solution, not Hamas. "We accepted that our state should be on the 1967 borders but Israel rejected that."[2] For too many reporters in the major media, however, once a person is labeled a "terrorist," they no longer feel compelled to accurately portray his views.

I had tried several times to interview Meshal during previous trips to Damascus, but he was either out of the country or in hiding due to a crisis with Israel. When we finally did meet, we found a most unexpected terrorist. Stocky, handsome, and with a neatly trimmed beard, Meshal could pass for an Arabic George Clooney. He speaks English comfortably and seems genuinely concerned with making himself understood to the outside world. He exudes charisma. But all those traits don't change the content of what he says. Even those opposed to Israeli policy will have sharp disagreements with Hamas, as do I. But the meeting was fascinating. And it finally happened most unexpectedly.

I WAS INVITED to a diplomatic reception for Bahrain's national day, the equivalent of July 4 for that tiny Persian Gulf kingdom. Diplomatic receptions are often boring affairs, and I almost didn't go. But free food is free food. I arrive at Damascus's Palace Restaurant, where major diplomatic receptions are often held. The room is full of fresh flowers, men with flowing white robes, and women with big hair. Formal events in Syria are a throwback to 1950s fashion. The women are either dressed with a hijab (headscarf) or look like hookers after a hard night's work—lots of eye shadow, mascara, and puffed-up hair. The men all look like Syria's former president Hafez al-Assad—short, gray, and sporting clipped mustaches. I fit right in.

The reception begins at seven o'clock, and buffet tables are piled high with Arabic hors d'oeuvres known as *mezza*. I want to snack, but our host says to wait. Not wanting to be an ugly American, I wait. I drink lots of tasty fruit juice, because no alcohol is served. I see waiters bring out savory rice, lamb, and roasted whole goat. The aromas are killing me. My stomach is rumbling, but I continue to wait. Then at precisely eight o'clock a band starts playing Arabic pop music on bagpipes. That's apparently a signal, because seconds later the hoards descend on the food tables. Remember when Peter O'Toole leads the Arab masses into battle against the Ottoman Turks in *Lawrence of Arabia*? The scene is recreated before my eyes, except the diplomats aren't chanting "Lawrence, Lawrence."

Diplomats in black tie elbow their way to the front of the line. A scrum of British surround the goat. Hamas stakes out a position near the fish. Hezbollah has the hummus. Peter and I cleverly walk over to the desert line, which is almost empty. I eat some excellent baklava and chocolate torte. By the time the line for the main course diminishes, however, we see nothing but cold rice and goat skulls.

While most famous as an actor in films such as *ET* and *Erin Brockovich*, Peter Coyote is also a talented writer. As a result of this trip, he was getting an intense, practical course in international journalism. He and I ended up writing an article for *Vanity Fair* about the failed U.S. raid on Syria in October 2008.[3] Peter brings some unexpected celebrity to the diplomatic reception. A waiter comes up and asks me a question in Arabic. (I told you I look like Hafez al-Assad.) He then repeats in English, "Your friend, I have seen him somewhere before?" That happens a lot to Peter. A gaggle of Syrian movie stars also attend the reception. One famous soap opera actress sports black hair curled around her ears, and wears green stockings and a tight-fitting, black leather bodice. She must be quite famous because everyone wants a picture taken with her. Then they recognize Peter. Suddenly all the Syrian soap opera stars want their picture taken with him, including green stockings.

Then we notice a minor commotion in the center of the room. Diplomats are swarming around a fit-looking man in an elegant suit. Khaled Meshal bristles with energy and good humor. But Meshal's bodyguards treat us as if we are potential assassins. As Peter edges in to hear better, the bodyguards wedge themselves between him and Meshal, always watching Peter's hands. Meshal is ever the gracious diplomat. He clasps my hand in both of his and says, "Welcome," as is the Arabic custom. He agrees immediately to our request for an interview, and with no apparent irony adds, "I am always happy to meet with Americans." He retrieves a business card from his wallet, scribbles a number on it, and hands it to us. For security reasons, he doesn't carry a cell phone, but the number will reach an aide.

ON THE APPOINTED DAY in December 2009, Peter and I are led into a reception room at the Hamas headquarters. We wait. And wait. And wait. We are working with a local Syrian journalist, who helps set up interviews and translates. She becomes restless, then agitated, and finally begins shouting at the bodyguards. "If Meshal doesn't appear quickly, we will leave," she exclaims. One security man says contemptuously, "You are journalists, you will wait." They may or may not be terrorists. But one thing is certain: yelling doesn't bother them.

Her shouting apparently has some impact, however, because Khaled Qadomi emerges. He heads Hamas's department of political relations. Speaking easily in English, he explains that a French TV crew has arrived late from the airport, and Meshal will meet us as soon as he completes that interview. Qadomi denies that Hamas is either a terrorist or a fundamentalist Muslim group, saying it is "a national liberation movement." Equating Hamas with the perpetrators of the 9/11 attack may grab headlines in the United States, he says, but it's not accurate. Al Qaeda seeks to create an authoritarian regime throughout the Muslim world. Hamas seeks the liberation of Palestine and works within its parliamentary system.[4] Before we have a chance for further discussion, the George Clooney of Palestine tells us he's ready for a close-up.

We change rooms, and a retinue of assistants, advisors, and security men file in, filling every easy chair in the ample space. We could be in polite company anywhere in the world, discussing politics without rancor or cant. Ever the Arab host, Meshal insists we have more coffee, and attendants deliver cookies and honeyed pastries made with delicate phyllo dough. Both Peter and I have met with many high-ranking government officials and film stars. Khaled Meshal ranks among the most impressive. He watches us intently until he has seen comprehension in our faces. If he does not, he stops and clarifies carefully. He makes a listener feel special, even as he spells out ideas with which we disagree.

Israel has used horrific violence against Palestinians, including dropping 500-pound bombs on apartment buildings to kill one Hamas leader. But does that justify Hamas using suicide bombers against Israeli civilians, or firing homemade rockets and mortars into civilian towns? Its charter calls for removing all Jews from Palestine. But Meshal is also a realist. The Israelis are not about to be pushed out of Palestine. Most Palestinians favor a two-state solution, in which an independent Palestine exists alongside Israel. So Hamas is willing to compromise. Meshal emphasizes to us that Hamas can live side-by-side with Israel if that country's leaders agree to international demands for an independent Palestinian state.[5]

Meshal points out that Hamas and *all* Palestinian political parties signed a national reconciliation statement in 2006, agreeing to a two-state solution if Israel returns to its 1967 borders, recognizes the right of Palestinian return, and agrees to a Palestinian state with Jerusalem as its capital. He says the United States should back such a solution. "If Obama wants peace," Meshal says mildly but with clear intent, "he must engage Hamas."[6] We talk about many other topics that day. The conversation continues through the afternoon and into the evening. His staff gives us large boxes filled with tiny Arab pastries and sweets. I'll explain more of what Meshal says, but first we need some more historical background.

HAMAS WAS FOUNDED in December 1987 by Sheik Ahmed Yassin and his followers as a branch of Egypt's Muslim Brotherhood. The Brotherhood had a long history in the Middle East as an anti-imperialist organization seeking to establish Arab governments ruled by a strict interpretation of Islam. The Brotherhood's views ran counter to the ideology and practice of most Palestinians at the time, and even today.

In 1987, the Palestinian movement had two main components. Fatah, led by Yasser Arafat, was a multi-class, nationalist organization, and had the support of a significant majority of the population. A number of leftist parties with Marxist origins provided an ideological alternative, but they represented a minority. Fatah, the leftist parties, independent nationalists, business people, prominent intellectuals, and others composed the Palestine Liberation Organization (PLO), which was recognized around the world as the legitimate representative of the Palestinian people.

From the beginning Hamas saw itself as a distinct, religious trend and refused to join the PLO. Hamas sought to merge a fundamentalist interpretation of Islam with anti-imperialism. "The Covenant of the Islamic Resistance Movement," Hamas's founding document, explicitly calls for an "Islamic Palestine" and criticizes the PLO for demanding a secular state. Rather pointedly it states, "The Islamic nature of Palestine is part of our religion and whoever takes his religion lightly is a loser." [7]

The secular PLO sought to unite all Palestinians, regardless of religion. Hamas pitched its appeal to Muslims, not Palestinian Christians or religious nonbelievers. Hamas leaders considered all of Palestine as an Islamic Waqf, or land held in trust for Muslims. Because

Palestine was conquered by Islam over 1300 years ago, their reasoning goes, it remains a Waqf today. "This Waqf remains as long as earth and heaven remain. Any procedure in contradiction to Islamic Sharia [religious law], where Palestine is concerned, is null and void."[8] Hamas's early ideology is a mirror image of right-wing Zionists who believed that all the territory from the Nile to the Euphrates (Egypt to Iraq) belongs to Jews because their biblical empire once occupied that territory.[9]

From the time that Yasser Arafat became PLO leader, the Palestinian movement made a distinction between Zionism as an ideology and the Jewish religion. Hamas's covenant makes no such distinction. The covenant is thoroughly anti-Jewish, not just anti-Zionist.[10] It distorts a particular quote from the Koran to justify fighting all Jews. The covenant reads, "The Prophet, Allah bless him and grant him salvation, has said: 'The Day of Judgment will not come about until Muslims fight the Jews, when the Jew will hide behind stones and trees. The stones and trees will say O Muslims, O Abdulla, there is a Jew behind me, come and kill him. Only the Gharkad tree, would not do that because it is one of the trees of the Jews.'"[11]

The covenant cites the "Protocols of the Elders of Zion" as if it were a real document rather than a forgery from Czarist Russia.[12] It goes on to present some truly bizarre, anti-Jewish conspiracy theories. Jews were responsible for the French Revolution, World War I, and the Bolshevik Revolution. "They were behind World War II, through which they made huge financial gains by trading in armaments, and paved the way for the establishment of their state. It was they who instigated the replacement of the League of Nations with the United Nations and the Security Council to enable them to rule the world through them. There is no war going on anywhere, without having their finger in it."[13]

Given Hamas's violent antagonism toward Jews, you would think the Israeli government would have immediately jailed Hamas leaders back in 1987. In fact, however, Israel allowed Sheik Yassin to freely operate his Islamic Center and accept funding from conservative Gulf State Arabs. Israel allowed Hamas to flourish in a cynical attempt to undercut the far more popular PLO.[14] Ironically, Israel does the same today, only now it favors Fatah over Hamas. Such tactics lead Palestinians to believe that Israel is not serious about negotiating with either group. Over the past 20 years Hamas has never renounced its covenant, but in practice it has changed its positions when confronted with Middle East realities. And one of the key figures leading that change is Khaled Meshal.

MESHAL WAS BORN IN 1956 in the West Bank village of Silwad, but his family moved to Kuwait after the 1967 war. His father was imam at a local mosque and sympathized with the politics of the Muslim Brotherhood. At age 15, Khaled joined the Brotherhood. He studied physics at Kuwait University and helped form an Islamic student group there. After Hamas was founded, Meshal joined and later became its leader in Kuwait. In 1990 Saddam Hussein's Iraq invaded Kuwait, and U.S. troops invaded the region in the first Gulf War. In 1991 Meshal left for Jordan, where he became head of Hamas in that country.

From 1987 to 1993 Palestinians waged the First Intifada, an unarmed uprising against Israeli occupation of the West Bank and Gaza. Palestinians held general strikes, refused to pay taxes, and boycotted Israeli goods. Palestinian youths frequently threw stones at Israeli Defense Forces (IDF) soldiers, who often responded with deadly force. The First Intifada convinced many Israelis that continuing occupation was too costly, both militarily and economically.

In the summer of 1993 Israel and the PLO announced an agreement that became known as the Oslo Peace Accords. On September 13, 1993, Prime Minister Yitzhak Rabin, PLO leader Yasser Arafat, and President Bill Clinton met in Washington to sign the accords.

Israel agreed to recognize a Palestinian Authority (PA) and withdraw some of its occupation troops. It allowed Arafat and other exiled leaders to return to the occupied territories. The PLO agreed to give up armed struggle, and accepted a two-state solution. For an interim period, the PA would control parts of the West Bank and Gaza, and Israel would continue to control the remainder and all of Jerusalem. Many details were left unresolved, and both sides agreed to negotiate a final agreement within five years.

Likud and other right-wing Israeli parties considered Oslo a sellout and maintained that all of Gaza and the West Bank should remain as Jewish land. They argued that the PLO didn't really accept a two-state solution and would use negotiations to impose a unitary, Palestinian state. On February 25, 1994—just five months after the Israeli Knesset (parliament) approved the Oslo Accords—right-wing settler Baruch Goldstein entered the mosque at Hebron's Cave of the Patriarchs with a Galil assault rifle. Dressed in an Israeli army uniform, he opened fire, murdering 29 Arab worshippers and injuring 125 others. Palestinians held demonstrations throughout the occupied territories. The IDF killed 19 protestors.[15] Clearly, sizeable factions in Israel were unwilling to accept Oslo and sanctioned violence to stop it.

Hamas, Islamic Jihad, and leftist Palestinian parties also opposed Oslo. They became collectively known as "rejectionists." They opposed a two-state solution in principle and argued that, in any case, the Israelis couldn't be trusted to negotiate a final agreement. Hamas began sporadic suicide bombings in 1993. It intensified the attacks after the Goldstein massacre in an effort to derail the Oslo peace process. In ensuing years, Hamas and other rejectionist groups attacked both military and civilian targets. Rejectionists fired mortars, launched homemade rockets, and carried out assassinations. Israel and the United States denounced all these activities as terrorism, whether carried out against civilians, soldiers, or Israeli government officials.[16]

In that regard, they followed the same protocol as British authorities who lambasted Zionists as terrorists prior to the 1948 independence of Israel.

From 1993 until halting the suicide bombing tactic in 2005, Hamas is credited with killing over 500 people in 350 attacks. In 2005 it renounced suicide bombings, and, as of this writing, none have occurred since.

By the early 1990s, Israel clearly saw Hamas as a serious threat. In 1997 Prime Minister Benyamin Netanyahu and his advisors decided to assassinate Khaled Meshal. The Israeli intelligence agency, Mossad, devised a deadly, untraceable toxin that could be squirted in the ear. Two agents traveled to Amman, Jordan, using false Canadian passports. On September 25 they planned to waylay Meshal, administer the poison, then flee without a trace. Instead, the conspiracy massively backfired.

When the agents attacked Meshal on the street, his bodyguard chased them down and had them arrested. When the full details of the assassination attempt came out, Jordan's King Hussein demanded that Israel provide an antidote or he would break relations with Israel. Israel not only provided the antidote, it had to release Hamas founder Sheik Yassin from prison. Meshal recovered and became internationally famous as a militant fighter against Israel.[17] In 2001 Meshal moved to Damascus, where he's given protection by the Syrian government. After the death of Sheik Yassin and another Hamas militant, Meshal became the top Hamas leader in 2004.

DURING THE EARLY 1990S, Hamas's popularity hovered around 20 percent, according to public opinion polls.[18] But after a right-winger assassinated Prime Minister Yitzhak Rabin in 1995, Israel ceased serious peace negotiations. The total number of Israeli settlers in Gaza, the West Bank, the Golan Heights, and East Jerusalem increased by 38 percent between 1993 and 2000.[19] Fatah, as the ruling group within the PA, proved to be corrupt and authoritarian. Hamas support began to grow, not so much because of its Islamist ideology but out of Palestinian frustration with Fatah and Israel.

The Second Intifada broke out in 2000 after Israeli opposition leader Ariel Sharon insisted on visiting the Al-Aqsa Mosque in Jerusalem, one of Islam's most holy sites. Sharon intentionally provoked the incident to show that Israel would never give up control of East Jerusalem, including the holy Islamic site. The Second Intifada lasted five years; over 1,000 Israelis and 5,500 Palestinians died.

After the collapse of Oslo and the rise of the Second Intifada, Hamas emerged with greater popular support. Hamas ran a populist campaign in the PA's parliamentary elections of January 2006. It accused Fatah of being a wealthy elite living off the backs of Palestinians. Hamas, its leaders said, was the legitimate inheritor of Palestinian nationalism. Hamas won a majority of the parliamentary seats and formed a new government in both the West Bank and Gaza.

The election results, although considered free and fair by international observers, were condemned by Israel and the United States.[20] Once again the United States proved to be a strong defender of democracy, except when the wrong people won. Western powers refused to recognize the Hamas government and sought to undermine it politically, economically, and militarily. The United States and Western Europe cut off aid to Hamas-controlled areas, and Israel tightened an economic blockade of Gaza, where Hamas had its strongest support.

Meshal strongly criticizes Israel and its allies for hypocrisy. "The day Hamas won the Palestinian democratic elections the world's leading democracies failed the test of democracy. Rather than recognize the legitimacy of Hamas as a freely elected representative of the Palestinian people, seize the opportunity created by the result to support the development of good governance in Palestine, and search for a means of ending the bloodshed, the U.S. and EU threatened the Palestinian people with collective punishment."[21]

Western interference had an impact. Fatah and Hamas engaged in armed clashes. After a series of skirmishes, Fatah seized control of the West Bank, and Hamas seized Gaza. Israel severely restricted food, medicine, fuel, and other essential goods from entering Gaza. It stopped all exports of Palestinian agricultural and industrial goods. The United Nations later created a special mission headed by former South African supreme court justice Richard Goldstone to investigate the Gaza conflict. The Goldstone Report indicates that the Israeli blockade intentionally degraded the operations of hospitals, the supply of water to homes, and sewage treatment. As a result, 80 percent of Gaza's drinking water didn't meet World Health Organization standards.[22]

Israel let in only enough goods to avert a humanitarian catastrophe. Israel hoped this collective punishment would convince Gazans to reject Hamas. Such policies, according to the Goldstone Report, constitute a "violation of international humanitarian law."[23] Meanwhile, Hamas and some other Palestinian groups continued to indiscriminately fire rockets and mortars into Israel. The groups launched an estimated 8,000 rockets from 2001 to 2008, killing and injuring civilians. The Goldstone Report found that the shelling caused physical and psychological injuries, particularly for children.

Hamas argues that it merely retaliates for Israeli attacks on Palestinian civilians. But deliberate targeting of civilians constitutes a crime against humanity, according to the Goldstone Report. "There is significant evidence to suggest that one of the primary purposes of the rocket and mortar attacks is to spread terror amongst the Israeli civilian population, a violation of international law."[24] Hamas initiated a ceasefire with Israel and stopped firing rockets beginning in July 2008. But Israel wasn't interested in a mere cessation of hostilities. It wanted to destroy Hamas as a military and political force. When the six-month ceasefire expired, Hamas asked for a lifting of the Gaza blockade as a condition for extending the truce. Israel refused. Hamas resumed firing rockets on December 18, 2008.

Many analysts believe that Israel didn't renew the ceasefire because it was waiting for an appropriate moment to attack.[25] Israel was headed into parliamentary elections in February. Prime Minister Ehud Olmert wanted to steal thunder from hard-right opposition leader Benyamin Netanyahu, who was demanding a crackdown on Hamas. The Israeli government was also sending a message to newly elected president Barack Obama that Israel, not the United States, controls the military situation in the region.

ON DECEMBER 27, 2008, the IDF bombed Gaza from the air. On January 3, 2009, Israeli troops launched a ground invasion. Although the Israeli government disputes the figures, the Goldstone Report found that 1,444 Palestinians died during the three weeks of fighting, mostly civilians. A total of four Israeli soldiers died in combat, and four Israelis (three civilians) were killed by Palestinian rockets. From the beginning, Israel exercised military supremacy in the war. Hamas leaders and fighters went into hiding to avoid confrontations they were bound to lose. But the Gaza War, like the 2006 Israeli invasion of Lebanon, can't be judged strictly in military terms.[26] The Israeli government sought to eliminate Hamas and return the more moderate Fatah to power. It sought to find and release Israeli corporal Gilad Shalit, who had been captured in 2006. It failed on both counts. Hamas's leadership and militia survived the Israeli onslaught and claimed victory.

Israeli leaders asserted they won the war because they degraded Hamas's ability to carry out terrorist attacks. They claimed to have targeted only Hamas military infrastructure and to have gone to great lengths to avoid civilian casualties. The IDF even made phone calls to residents in apartment buildings where Hamas members lived to give them time to evacuate prior to air raids on the buildings. But the rest of the world saw a far different picture. Israel was applying what its military leaders call the "Dahiya doctrine." It involves, according to the Goldstone Report, "the application of disproportionate force and the causing of great damage and destruction to civilian property and infrastructure, and suffering to civilian populations."[27]

For example, making prerecorded calls to Palestinian apartment residents and dropping leaflets were meaningless gestures because civilians had no safe place to seek shelter. Numerous UN personnel witnessed indiscriminate bombings and shelling of civilian targets. The IDF intentionally targeted hospitals and ambulances.[28] The IDF destroyed the Palestinian parliament building, the Al Quds Hospital, and the Gaza City jail, claiming they were part of the "Hamas infrastructure." The IDF also used white phosphorous bombs to attack a UN Relief and Works Agency (UNRWA) facility housing 600–700 Palestinian refugees. The use of white phosphorous is particularly horrific because it causes untreatable burns. The Geneva Conventions prohibit the use of white phosphorous against civilian targets.[29] In January 2010, the Israeli government paid the United Nations $10.5 million in compensation for destruction of its facilities during the Gaza War but continued to claim the damage was accidental.[30]

NOT LOSING, HOWEVER, doesn't mean winning. Hamas emerged from the 2009 Gaza War chastened. It stopped almost all rocket attacks for a year and didn't resume suicide bombings, an implicit admission of Israeli military strength. While it continues to defend the use of armed resistance, in practice, Hamas focuses on political survival. Hamas has modified its stands without formally changing its founding documents. Even several years before the war, Hamas was already changing its views.

After the 2006 parliamentary elections, Khaled Meshal launched an international effort to portray Hamas as a responsible national liberation organization that believed in armed struggle rather than religious war. He met with top Egyptian and Russian leaders. Meshal even made a positive impression during meetings with retired U.S. diplomats. Edward Peck, former U.S. ambassador to Iraq, told the London *Times* that Meshal is a "'moderate in many senses,' willing to engage in dialogue with Washington. 'These guys were entirely rational. They are not wild-eyed shrieking whackos.'"[31]

Meshal also sharply changed the group's view of Jews as compared to the 1988 Hamas covenant. In a commentary for the British *Guardian* newspaper, Meshal wrote, "Our message to the Israelis is this: we do not fight you because you belong to a certain faith or culture. Jews have lived in the Muslim world for 13 centuries in peace and harmony . . . Our conflict with you is not religious but political. We have no problem with Jews who have not attacked us—our problem is with those who came to our land, imposed themselves on us by force, destroyed our society and banished our people . . . If you are willing to accept the principle of a long-term truce, we are prepared to negotiate the terms."[32]

Even former Mossad (Israeli intelligence) chief Ephraim Halevy admits Hamas has undergone significant changes "right under our very noses. Its ideological goal is not attainable and will not be in the foreseeable future." Ephraim writes that Hamas will accept a two-state solution within the 1967 borders.[33] Most Israeli leaders ignore Hamas's changed positions, however, arguing that Hamas must fully accept Israel as a Jewish state before they will be willing to recognize a Palestinian state. This is a relatively new demand. Earlier Israeli governments never asked the PLO to accept Israel as a Jewish state. Palestinian leaders, including Fatah, won't accept such a demand because it means codifying an unequal status for Palestinians living in Israel, not to mention eliminating any possibility of the right of exiled Palestinians to return.[34]

It seems inevitable that one day Israel will be forced to acknowledge Hamas's changing views, as it did with the PLO. Hamas is willing to live with Israel, Meshal tells us, if Israel meets its obligations to Palestinians. If Palestinians support a two-state solution, he tells me, "Hamas will respect the majority opinion and would then decide if its own position would be for a one- or two-state solution." The PLO went through a similar process in the 1980s. The PLO charter, written in 1963, called for destroying the state of Israel and creating a secular Palestinian state in its place. In the early 1980s, Yasser Arafat concluded that such an option was unrealistic and came to favor a two-state solution. But the PLO charter wasn't formally changed until 1996.

WE CAN LEARN A LOT about how Hamas might govern a future Palestinian state by looking at how it runs Gaza today. Hamas has been the ruling authority in Gaza since July 2007, when it kicked out the Fatah-controlled security forces and civil servants. Any group would have trouble governing Gaza under the severe economic, political, and military restraints Israel imposes. The outlines of Hamas policy have emerged nevertheless.

Gaza is a thin strip of land hard up against the Mediterranean Sea. After the 1948 war, Palestinians fled to Gaza, which was then controlled by Egypt. After the 1967 war, Israel seized Gaza, along with the West Bank. Over time, Israel faced mounting casualties from guerrilla warfare and was unable to control the Palestinian population. The Israeli government unilaterally withdrew from Gaza in 2005. However, Israel continues to control all access from sea, air, and land.

Hamas governs a tiny territory of 139 square miles with a pop-

ulation of about 1.5 million. Most of the population depends on
UN shipments for food and other essentials. The United States and
Europe, which had been providing aide to the Palestinian Authority
in Gaza, cut off all funds. The most dynamic portion of the Gaza
economy is the building of tunnels used to smuggle food, medicine,
fuel, and arms—all at inflated prices.

Even under these difficult conditions, Hamas has maintained
some level of popular support. The previous government headed by
Fatah was notorious for requiring bribes to obtain government contracts and for other forms of corruption. Hamas put a stop to such
practices. Police are considered honest. Hamas's Ministry of National
Economy offers interest-free, small business loans; the Public Works
Ministry repaves roads; the Finance Ministry collects taxes—all without the previous corruption. The Hamas government Web site lists
administration appointments and rules, providing much more trans-
parency than in the past.[35] The Local Affairs Ministry even regulates
tunnel building.

Hamas has decided not to create an Islamic state in Gaza, whether
due to a change in ideology or for expediency. But some Palestinians see that decision as a sellout and want to impose a strict version
of Sharia law that would execute apostates and stone adulterers.[36]
Such fundamentalist groups in Gaza pose a threat to Hamas. An
organization called the Army of Islam kidnapped BBC reporter
Alan Johnston, even though he had been critical of Israeli policies.
In July 2007 Hamas's Qassem Brigades attacked an Army of Islam
stronghold and freed Johnston. In August 2009 another group, the
Warriors of God, took over a mosque in the southern Gaza city of
Rafah. The Warriors of God claimed Hamas is not Islamic enough
and that it collaborates with Israel.[37] On August 14, Hamas security
forces attacked the mosque and crushed the uprising. According to
the Palestine Centre for Human Rights, 28 Palestinians were killed
and over 100 wounded during the attack.[38]

In response to pressure from such fundamentalist groups, Hamas's Religious Endowments Ministry formed a morals police to "propagate virtue and prevent vice." It tells residents not to mix the sexes, not to touch one another on the beach, and to adhere to austere dress codes. But it's not clear if all the Hamas leadership supports such measures. Schools imposed stringent dress codes that were later rescinded. When Islamic Courts in Gaza required female lawyers to wear the hijab, Hamas's prime minister Ismail Haniya had the rule reversed.[39] Tensions exist within the Hamas leadership on this question.

Hamas has managed to cut down on corruption and maintain stability under very difficult conditions. But that's not the same as governing democratically. Hamas rules with a strong hand and tolerates little dissent. For all its problems, the Palestinian Authority in the West Bank still seeks to build consensus among Palestinian groups. Moderate and leftist opponents can organize openly. Hamas allows no such opposition.

A Human Rights Watch report accuses Hamas of killing at least 32 opponents during the Israeli invasion of Gaza in December–January 2008 9. It illegally detained and tortured dozens more. "Masked gunmen beat and maimed by shooting dozens of Hamas's political opponents, especially members and supporters of its main political rival, Fatah,"[40] Human Rights Watch wrote. "It is difficult to determine whether or not the abuses documented in this report resulted from a policy decision by Hamas leaders, but the extent and frequency of the violations strongly suggests such a policy. At the very least, Hamas security forces are not doing enough to prevent or punish these abuses."[41]

KHALED MESHAL REMAINS the leader of a group committed to armed struggle to liberate Palestine. In its early years, Hamas used terrorist tactics in hopes of establishing an Islamic state. But Hamas has evolved since 1987. A sizeable majority of Palestinians favor a secular rather than an Islamic state. Fatah, despite its corruption and authoritarian habits, retains significant popular support. Israel will undoubtedly remain the dominant military power in the region for the foreseeable future. Pragmatic Hamas leaders such as Meshal recognize these realities and are changing their views accordingly.

Like the PLO and Hezbollah, Hamas has had to confront the reality of governing in a Middle East where its allies have little power compared to the United States and Israel. Iran provides an estimated $20–30 million per year to Hamas, and Hamas receives money from Islamic charities around the world. But Iran can't send tanks or missiles to Hamas because of the Israeli blockade. Although Hamas continues to use the rhetoric of armed struggle, it can't deal crushing military blows to Israel.

But the Palestinians can force Israel to compromise politically. Former prime minister Olmert finally admitted that Israeli hard-line policies could never bring peace. He called for creating a Palestinian state on land captured by Israel before 1967, with East Jerusalem as its capital, and for returning the Golan Heights to Syria.[42] No important Israeli leader had ever acknowledged the legitimacy of the Palestinian position before. Unfortunately, Olmert did it only when he was leaving office due to a financial scandal. But he set a precedent for future Israeli leaders who want to face reality.

For the moment, Israel has the upper hand and has refused to engage in meaningful negotiations. But if Fatah and Hamas can resolve their differences, a combination of internal and international pressure can alter Israeli policies. Shawan Jabarin, head of the Al Haq human rights organization in Ramallah, tells me that both Palestinians and Israelis will eventually have to negotiate a solution based on two states living in peace. "In the near future, I have no hope," he says. "For mid- and long-term, I believe we will build peace. The

Israelis can't kill all Palestinians. And the Palestinians can't kill all the Israelis." [43]

Hamas will remain a viable force within Palestinian politics for some time. Eventually, Israeli leaders will stop calling Hamas "terrorists" as they did with the PLO. After all, early Zionist groups used the same kinds of tactics. In the next chapter, we'll look at the long history of what some call Jewish terrorism.

GEULA COHEN,
member of Stern Gang and former member
of the Israeli parliament
Photo credit: Reese Erlich

three

Geula Cohen: Jewish Terrorist?

IT'S FITTING THAT GEULA COHEN lives in the French Hill section of East Jerusalem on a mountain not far from where the prophet Jeremiah stayed. Before 1967, East Jerusalem was part of Jordan; today French Hill is all Israeli. So Geula Cohen, grand dame of the Israeli Right, lives on land once owned by Arabs that may have been previously owned by Jews 3,400 years ago.

Cohen welcomes me into her modest apartment on a side street in a middle-income neighborhood. She wears a red print shift and house slippers. Her hair is slightly mussed. The once raven-haired beauty has become a somewhat overweight, Jewish grandmother. At age 84, Cohen has slowed down considerably. On this day, she walks hesitantly and painfully because of recent back surgery. But she's mentally alert and as outspoken as ever.

In the 1940s Cohen joined the Stern Gang, a group that proudly used terrorist tactics against British colonial officials. She acknowledges that Zionist groups used terrorism against Palestinians in Israel's 1948 War of Independence. Cohen helped found the ultrarightist Israeli settlers' movement in the 1970s and was elected to the Knesset (Israeli parliament) as leader of an ultranationalist party. As we went over her entire political history, she never once expressed a change of view, let alone any regret. She is truly a True Believer.

Yet many Israelis, even progressives, hold her in high esteem. She cohosts a popular weekly radio program and has the reputation of an intellectual. She says she reads the Bible and poetry every night before bed. Even sharp critics admire that she has stuck to her principles. And at a time when recent Israeli prime ministers have faced corruption investigations, Cohen has remained honest. Her apartment is filled with photos and paintings; the dining room table is piled high with papers and magazines. But there are no outward signs of wealth. She lives modestly, as she has for years. Cohen even gets grudging praise from Ms. Ronny Perlman, a leader in Machsom (Checkpoint) Watch, a grassroots Israeli women's movement that defends Palestinian rights. "Since we have so many corrupt politicians, people have some kind of weak spot for her. She was always very faithful to her ideas and never changed camps, which many of our politicians have done."[1]

But political consistency and lack of corruption hasn't enhanced Cohen's stature among Palestinians. In random interviews with people on the street, as well as with leaders, Palestinians universally expressed hatred of Cohen. They remember her close association with Gush Emunim (Block of the Faithful), a settler group that drove many Palestinians out of the city of Hebron in the 1980s. "She and people like her initiated a fascist trend in Israel," says Mustafa Barghouthi, a moderate member of the Palestinian legislature and former presidential candidate. "Her advocacy of discrimination and racism has become the basis of segregation in the occupied territories."[2]

Just in case you weren't sure if Geula Cohen qualifies as a terrorist, please note the title of her 1966 book published in the United States as *Woman of Violence: Memoirs of a Terrorist 1943–1948*. So who is this Geula Cohen, and what does her current status tell us about Israeli-Palestinian relations today?

GEULA COHEN WAS BORN in Tel Aviv in 1925, a tumultuous era by any measure. After World War I, Britain and France split up the territory of the defeated Ottoman Empire. Britain created the Mandate of Palestine, which consisted of what today includes Israel, West Bank, Gaza Strip, and part of Jordan. The British had an impeccable flair for divide and conquer tactics, promising the same land to local Arabs, to the Hashemite King of Jordan, and to the Zionists. During the 1920s and '30s, the British colonialists ruled the Middle East with an iron fist, frequently pitting Arabs and Jews against one another to maintain their rule.

By the eve of World War II, two major Zionist groups had emerged to fight militarily against British colonialism. The largest was the Haganah (The Defense), whose members went on to form the Labor Party. The smaller group was Etzel, also known as Irgun (National Military Organization), the paramilitary forerunner of Likud and other right-wing parties. Both movements agreed to not fight the British during World War II as part of the larger struggle against Nazi Germany. Some ultranationalists from Etzel denounced this stand as collaborationist, however, and broke away to form Lechi (Fighters for the Freedom of Israel), led by Abraham (Yair) Stern. In 1943 Geula Cohen joined Lechi, also known as the Stern Gang, the most nationalist and violent of the Zionist groups. It called for establishing an independent country in the territory once occupied by ancient Israel, "from the Nile to the Euphrates" (that is, from Egypt to Iraq). The Stern Gang bombed and assassinated British police, soldiers, and government officials.

Lechi argued that Germany and Britain were equally evil, and therefore Zionists should continue the armed struggle against the British during the war. As Cohen wrote in her memoir about the World War II years, "The only way to save the Jews of the Diaspora was to create an independent homeland, deprive the English of their power. Between master and slave there could be no cease fire. There could only be war."[3]

Cohen writes romantically about a female Lechi member who unsuccessfully attempted to assassinate British general Evelyn Barker by planting explosives in a baby carriage. "She hurried toward him, not running—just pushing a baby carriage . . . The baby in the carriage, however, was a doll with a dynamite body and a detonator for a heart."[4] If Palestinians used such tactics today to attack an IDF general, Israelis would be outraged. But Lechi considered such tactics legitimate against the British. In one of its more celebrated murders, two Lechi members in Cairo assassinated Lord Moyne, the British minister of state for the Middle East. That attack proved too much for the mainstream Zionist leaders in Palestine. The Haganah rounded up the perpetrators and handed them over to the British.

Cohen didn't participate in armed actions directly, but not for lack of trying. She told me she wanted to carry arms but couldn't effectively use the heavy bolt action rifles. But she considered herself a revolutionary and ultimately became known for reading propaganda broadcasts over Lechi's clandestine radio. Even today Cohen defends all Lechi's terrorist acts. "Every movement for freedom throughout history was forced to use means of force, guns and so on," she tells me, "because when you are a minority, you can't fight the government face-to-face."[5]

Cohen and other supporters of Lechi argue that terrorism was justified as part of the anti-colonial struggle. "Lechi always admitted they were terrorists, but terrorists for a good cause," says Yair Stern. He's the son of the late Avraham Stern and a former head of Israeli state TV. "They never intentionally hurt civilians. They did terrorist acts but against the police and army of British rule. Sometimes civilians were hurt, but it wasn't on purpose."[6]

In reality, however, Lechi did much more. At least half its victims were Jews accused of being British collaborators. And, as we'll see, within a few short years they turned their terrorist wrath against the United Nations and the Palestinians. But perhaps the most revealing example of extreme nationalism came in 1941 when Avraham Stern offered to collaborate with the Germans. "My father sent a messenger to meet the German ambassador in Damascus," Yair Stern told me, "and give him a letter that suggested Lechi will help the Germans by fighting the British if the Germans will allow Jews to get out of Europe. The letter was given to the ambassador, but there was no answer."

The extreme right-wing nationalism conveyed in the offer is shocking. Had the plan been accepted, or indeed had Lechi succeeded in weakening the British through terrorist actions, the consequences would have been devastating for Jews, Arabs, and the whole world. At the time, the vast majority of Jews opposed the Stern Gang. What good would it do to defeat the British in Palestine if it led to Hitler's control of the Middle East? Even Cohen admits in her memoirs that Lechi lacked popular support and had a hard time finding civilians to aid them.[7]

But after the end of World War II, Lechi found a new life as *all* the Zionist groups intensified their armed actions against the British and later against Arabs.

- In 1946 Irgun bombed the King David Hotel, the British headquarters in Jerusalem. The bomb killed a total of 90 Arabs, Jews, and British officials.[8]
- On January 5, 1948, Irgun packed shrapnel into 50-gallon oil drums and blew up 17 Arab civilians at the Jaffa Gate of the old city of Jerusalem.[9]
- That same night, the Haganah suspected that Arabs had established a headquarters in the Semiramis Hotel in Jerusalem. Two operatives blew up the building's support beams and killed 26 people, including guests and a Spanish diplomat.[10]

Faced with hostile Arab and Jewish populations, Britain ultimately had to station 100,000 troops in Palestine. Weakened by World War II and facing competition from the United States, the

British Empire was crumbling. Britain agreed to withdraw its troops from Palestine by May 1948. For Yair Stern and many other Israelis, the lesson was clear: terrorism works. "If you look back at history," he tells me, "the casualties to the British Army and police here in Israel, this is what made the British leave the country. British women were demonstrating against the government, saying 'Bring our boys home.' Finally, the British government caved under popular opinion."

But the end of British rule didn't stop the terrorism.

AS THE DATE FOR BRITISH WITHDRAWAL approached, the United Nations negotiated a partition plan that would give roughly half the land to Palestinian Arabs and half to the Zionists, with the United Nations administering Jerusalem as an international city. Neither Arab nor Zionist leaders really wanted partition, although the Haganah formally agreed to it. Lechi rejected partition outright and insisted that the Zionists control all of Mandatory Palestine, including Jerusalem. When UN mediator Count Folke Bernadotte continued to advocate partition, the Stern Gang decided to assassinate him. The murder was planned and approved by Stern Gang leader Yitzhak Shamir, later to become prime minister. Cohen's future husband, Immanuel Hanegbi, was also suspected of planning the operation. On September 17, 1948, Lechi members in Jerusalem fired a Thompson submachine gun at point blank range, murdering Bernadotte and a UN aide.

In our interview, Cohen continues to justify the assassination because Bernadotte advocated that Jerusalem be controlled by the United Nations rather than the Zionists. "For 2,000 years we were longing for our capital, and so we wanted to stop him, we tried to tell him if he would not stop his policy, he would be stopped physically. I was sent all of a sudden to Jerusalem to broadcast. They [Lechi leaders] wanted to make it more dramatic. They sent me to say [he should] leave Jerusalem, go to your Oslo, but two days later, he was killed."

Bernadotte was, in fact, Swedish, not Norwegian. But his murder made it even more difficult for the United Nations to negotiate a political settlement. Cohen told me that although he publicly opposed the Bernadotte assassination, David Ben-Gurion told her privately that he approved. I was unable to confirm that assertion from other sources. Ben-Gurion went on to become Israel's first, and perhaps most famous, prime minister. In later years, "I was very close to him [Ben-Gurion] as a friend," Cohen told me. "I know that he was very much satisfied. Afterwards he understood it was the salvation of Jerusalem."[11]

The Stern Gang's brand of terror tactics and nationalism were perfectly consistent. Jews have been oppressed for thousands of years, they argued, and their only salvation is the creation of a Jewish state. Anyone who stands in their way becomes a legitimate military target, whether British colonialists, Jews they deem collaborators, UN officials, or Arabs. "Whatever benefits the nation, even if it brings harm to many individuals, is morally desirable," Cohen writes. "Whatever brings harm to the nation, even if it proves a blessing to many individuals, is morally undesirable."[12] Such nationalism, once at the extreme end of the Israeli political spectrum, has today become part of the mainstream. And that consensus began to develop during Israel's fight against the Palestinians in the late 1940s.

ISRAELIS DECLARED INDEPENDENCE in May 1948. Many local Palestinians and leaders of neighboring Arab countries saw the Jews as an alien, Western colonial force introduced into Palestine by the British. Even David Ben-Gurion wrote during the 1936–39 Arab uprising against the British that Arabs have legitimate anger against the Zionists. "The country is theirs because they inhabit it, whereas we want to come here and settle down."[13]

Arab opposition to British imperialism intermingled with hatred of Jews, and some of the more extremist Arab leaders called for driving Jews into the sea. But just as the Zionists held differing political views, so did the Arabs. Mohammad Amin al-Husayni, the Grand Mufti of Jerusalem, was a right-wing nationalist who moved to Berlin during World War II. He encouraged Muslims to support the Axis war effort. On the other hand, some 6,000 Palestinian Arabs joined the British armed forces and fought the Nazis alongside Jewish volunteers.

After the declaration of Israeli independence in 1948, many local Palestinians joined with armies from Egypt, Iraq, Lebanon, Jordan, and Syria to fight Israel. Arab forces engaged in regular warfare as well as terrorist attacks in an effort to drive Jews out of Palestine.

- On February 1, 1948, Arab partisans lit the fuse on a car bomb parked in front of the *Palestine Post* newspaper building in Jerusalem, killing three civilians.
- On February 22, the Arab High Command carried out a TNT bombing attack on Ben Yehuda Street in a Jewish section of Jerusalem. Fifty-four civilians were murdered.[14]
- On March 11, 1948, Arab fighters planted a car bomb at the Jewish Agency in Jerusalem, the institution responsible for bringing Jews to Palestine. Thirteen civilian employees of the agency died.[15]

Such attacks grabbed headlines, but they served only to strengthen Jewish resolve to fight what was seen as a second holocaust. Left-wing writer Uri Avnery, who later became a leading peace advocate, enlisted to fight in the 1948 war. "We were totally convinced that we were faced with the danger of annihilation and that we were defending ourselves, our families, and the entire Hebrew community."[16] Initially the Jewish state was indeed imperiled militarily. But the Arab armies were disorganized and poorly armed. Israel was supported internationally by both the United States and the Soviet Union. In June 1948 there was a temporary armistice, during which the Israeli

forces received advanced weapons from Soviet-allied Czechoslovakia. Fighting soon resumed and Israelis took the military offensive.
According to UN figures, Mandatory Palestine had a total population
of 1,845,000 people, comprised of 67 percent Arab and 33 percent
Jews.[17] If Israel was to exist as a Zionist state, a homeland for the Jews,
Zionist leaders wondered what was to be done about the overwhelming number of Arabs?

Official Israeli history declares that during the 1948 war Arabs
fled voluntarily or at the behest of Arab leaders. Some did leave of
their own accord with the expectation of returning soon. But the
Zionist militias also used terror tactics to intimidate and ultimately
drive out most of the Arab population during the war of 1948–49.
The separate militias run by the Haganah, Irgun, and Lechi increasingly cooperated with one another, and in June 1948 they merged to
form the Israeli Defense Forces, or IDF. Seizing the military initiative,
the combined Israeli militias bombed Palestinian villages, forcing
residents to flee. Avnery offers a balanced view of what happened
next. "In the second half of the war, after the advance of the Arab
armies was halted, a deliberate policy of expelling the Arabs became
a war aim on its own."[18]

The Lechi dream of conquering territory and "transferring" (that
is, expelling) the Arab population became the de facto policy of all
the Zionist groups.

The massacre in the Arab village of Deir Yassin became the most
notorious example of this policy. Ironically, Deir Yassin residents
had good relations with a neighboring Jewish kibbutz (farm collective), whose leaders had guaranteed that the Arab villagers wouldn't
be attacked. But Deir Yassin residents lived near the crucial road to
Jerusalem, and the Haganah ordered the village seized. The attack
was carried out by the Stern Gang and Irgun. On April 9, 1948, the
militias met unexpectedly stiff armed resistance from local villagers.
Even after the fighting stopped, however, the militias went door-to-

door killing Arab men, women, and children. Arab prisoners were taken to Jerusalem in chains and publicly executed. Over 260 civilians died that day.[19]

Geula Cohen still defends her militia's actions at Deir Yassin. The Palestinians "were fighting; we asked if they would come out of their homes. We didn't want to kill them. They didn't leave their houses, and they fought us."[20] That version of events is directly contradicted by Jacques de Reynier, who worked for the International Red Cross and visited Deir Yassin three days after the massacre. In official reports, he documented numerous cases of atrocities committed by Zionist militia members, including assaults and rapes of local women.[21]

Dozens of similar, but less publicized attacks also took place. In recent years progressive Israeli historians have documented these massacres that had long been reported by Palestinians. Terror attacks against civilians occurred in Palestinian villages such as Nasr al-Din, Ain al-Zeitouneh, al-Bina, al-Bassa, and Safsaf.[22] Traditional Israeli historians reject such accounts as fabrications or exaggerations by Palestinian witnesses. For the sake of argument, let's say that no such massacres ever took place and that Palestinians fled at the behest of Arab leaders. Then why didn't the IDF allow some of the roughly 750,000 Palestinians to return to their homes? The official argument was that they posed a security threat. But Deir Yassin showed that even Arabs who allied with the Zionists weren't considered safe.

In reality, the new state of Israel couldn't survive as a Jewish state with too many Palestinians within its borders. As Avnery, then fighting with a commando unit of the IDF, writes, "We had received orders to kill every Arab who tried to return home." When pressed, Geula Cohen admitted to me that all the Zionist militias intentionally drove the Palestinians off their land. "Ben-Gurion encouraged the commanders of the army to try to get rid of them, not by killing, but get them to run away," she says. I ask, "How did you get them to run away?" "It's a problem; when their choice is to be killed or run away, they run away."[23]

By the end of the 1948 war, Israel had increased its territory by 45 percent over the size of the proposed UN partition. In each successive war, Israel was to similarly expand. In 1948, the remainder of what was supposed to be a Palestinian state was taken by Jordan; Egypt came to control the Gaza Strip. Israel later seized those territories in the 1967 war. Today Israel occupies almost all of Mandatory Palestine.

After the 1948 war until the mid-1970s, the Labor Party dominated Israeli politics. Then, former Irgun head and leader of the right-wing Likud party, Menachem Begin became prime minister from 1977–83. He resigned and turned over the post to former Stern Gang leader Yitzhak Shamir, who held the job in 1983–84 and 1986–92. With time, the pre-1948 tactical differences faded.

Today Lechi is an officially recognized and honored liberation organization. It has a museum, and streets in Jerusalem and Tel Aviv are named for Avraham Stern. Since 1980 the IDF has offered to award a "Lechi Fighter for the Freedom of Israel" ribbon to anyone who served in the group for at least six months. Yair Stern says Lechi today is part of the Israeli political consensus. "With time that has passed, people look at things differently," he tells me. "It also changed because of demographics. Most Israelis were born here after 1948 or emigrated from other countries. They look at history differently."

For Israel, yesterday's terrorists are today's heroes.

AFTER ISRAEL'S INDEPENDENCE Geula Cohen worked for many years as a reporter. She became famous for her in-depth interviews with both political and cultural figures. She married her wartime compatriot Immanuel Hanegbi, and in 1957 their son Tzhai Hanegbi was born. Today the younger Hanegbi is a member of the Knesset from the conservative Kadima Party. But Geula Cohen never gave up her political activism and beliefs. In 1967 Israel defeated three Arab countries and seized the Golan Heights from Syria, the West Bank from Jordan, and the Gaza Strip and Sinai desert from Egypt. Israel was one step closer to Cohen's old dream of a biblical kingdom from the Nile to the Euphrates.

The official Israeli position at the time was that it would exchange "land for peace," which meant that if the Arab countries agreed to diplomatically recognize Israel and live peacefully, Israel would return the occupied territories. At the time, however, Arab countries were unwilling to recognize Israel, and the Palestinian national movement was too weak to assert its own demands. In the years to follow, however, Israeli leaders showed that they didn't intend to return most of the captured territory. In 1967 Israeli leaders faced the same problem as the Zionist movement had in 1948: the occupied territories were full of Arabs. For 10 years after the 1967 war, the left of center Labor Party encouraged Jewish settlements in the Golan Heights, West Bank, and Gaza. After the election of conservative Menachem Begin as prime minister in 1977, the floodgates opened even wider.

Once again, Geula Cohen jumped into the fray. In 1974 she helped organize Gush Emunim, an extremist settler group. Gush Emunim rabbis Moshe Levinger and Eliezer Waldman founded the settlement of Kiryat Arba near Hebron in the West Bank. In the early '80s, Jewish settlers forced their way into central Hebron and established a small encampment in the middle of the Palestinian city. The Gush Emunim tactics became a model for other settlers. They applied to the Israeli government to build settlements on vacant land. Or they illegally moved trailers onto land in Palestinian neighborhoods. After some confrontations with the government, the authorities caved in and legalized those settlements as well.

When I first visited Hebron in 1987 on assignment for the *San Francisco Chronicle*, Gush Emunim occupied four contiguous buildings in the center of the old city. When I returned in 2009, they had displaced hundreds more Palestinians and controlled a mile-long strip and a hillside enclave. I first interviewed Cohen in Hebron in 1987.

She very clearly stated that the purpose of the settlements was to fore-stall the formation of a Palestinian state. "The settlements are closing the hope of the Palestinians that one day they can have a state."[24]

In a 2009 interview, Shawan Jabarin, director of the Al Haq human rights organization in Ramallah, told me that Hebron settlers want to evacuate parts of the old city. "They are trying to build a corridor between Hebron and Kiryat Arba to permanently split the city."[25] Cohen confirms that "it is not a goal which is officially announced, but that's the reality."[26] When necessary the settlers use terrorist tactics to expel Palestinian residents. If a single Palestinian attacks a settler, the IDF retaliates against his family or an entire neighborhood. For example, over a period of months, the once-thriving Arab market next to the Jewish settlement was closed down and blocks of Arab streets became no-man's-land after troops shut down Arab shops.

Even this harsh treatment isn't enough for the Jews living in Hebron, most of whom are from the United States. David Wilder, spokesperson for the Jewish Community of Hebron, told me that if teenage Palestinians continue to throw rocks at settlers after one warning, they should be "expelled to Lebanon."[27] Although many Israelis consider the Hebron residents to be extremists, the settlers nevertheless enjoy Israeli government protection. As of this writing, a total of 90 settler families live with a permanent guard of 2,000 soldiers. MachsomWatch leader Perlman told me the Hebron settlers have become more acceptable to Israeli political leaders with the passage of time. "There has never been any serious effort to dismantle the illegal settlements in Hebron by any government," she said.

THE SETTLEMENT ISSUE has become a flashpoint for peace talks between Israeli and Palestinian leaders. Today some 300,000 Israelis live in the West Bank and another 200,000 in Arab East Jerusalem. In 2009 I drove from Jerusalem to Tel Aviv using the settler roads reserved strictly for Israelis. The modern highway passed numerous settlements where Jews moved to get less expensive housing. But Palestinians are not allowed to cross the roads, even on foot, except through military checkpoints. A farmer with a house on one side and his farmland on the other is completely dependent on the Israeli army to get to work each day.

The settlements take up some of the best land in the West Bank. When Israeli leaders discuss a possible peace agreement, they always insist that certain settlements and their access roads remain inside Israeli territory. But it is precisely those settlements that constitute impenetrable barriers to a viable Palestinian state. "That was the idea," admits Yair Stern. He tells me that army general and then prime minister "Ariel Sharon, who masterminded the whole settler movement, put the settlements in such a way that they crisscrossed the West Bank so that in the future it won't be possible to have a independent Palestinian state, or it would be very difficult to do it." To this day, Cohen remains proud of her role in helping establish the illegal settlements in Hebron. "In Hebron and Kiryat Arba are the only free people in our country," she says.

Palestinian leader Barghouthi tells me Cohen's actions in 1948 and the 1980s remain consistent. "She did not see a difference between terrorist acts in 1948 and what she did in politics later. These are hard-core people who are extremists, who could not understand that there is a better way to have security for Israel, which is peace with the Palestinians rather than continuous oppression."

NOT SURPRISINGLY, COHEN HAS OPPOSED every peace plan in recent memory. As a member of the Knesset she even voted against the 1978 Camp David Accords in which Egypt signed a peace treaty in return for getting back the Sinai. The treaty removed Egypt as a potential military threat to Israel and serves as a model that some in Israel hope to use for peace treaties with other Arab neighbors. Cohen argues that

Egypt, even without the treaty, was not a military threat to Israel. She gets a dreamy look in her eye speculating what would have happened if Israel had allowed the IDF and hundreds of Jewish settlers to keep control of Sinai. Interestingly enough, she doesn't talk about it as a biblical land once inhabited by Jews. "Imagine that we could stay there, and we would have all the oil, and the military facilities."

Cohen continues to believe that Palestinians should not have an independent state in any part of the West Bank or Gaza. Palestinians have their own state, she argues, Jordan. I ask her about Prime Minister Netanyahu's declaration in 2009, under pressure from the Obama administration, that Israel is willing to hold negotiations to form a Palestinian state. She smiles and notes that Netanyahu pretends to negotiate, for international consumption, but won't make concessions acceptable to Palestinians. "That's essentially what Netanyahu is doing. [He offers] talks without preconditions, but he knows they are not going to go anywhere."

GEULA COHEN is an old woman now. But she remains intellectually sharp and fully aware of her history. In some ways I understand Israelis' ambivalence about this larger-than-life character. Her era spans the critical periods of Israeli history, and she's outlasted many of her enemies. She has a friendly and straightforward demeanor. During my interviews with her, there is no artifice: just blunt opinions. Yair Stern sums up the feelings of her political supporters when he tells me, "I wish she would live forever. I don't see anyone taking her place. She's one of a kind."

But I'm afraid history will make a much harsher judgment. As Palestinian leader Barghouthi tells me, "Unfortunately her contribution to politics was extremely negative. I hope the Israeli public will wake up one day and discover that these ideas of racism do not have a place in the 21st century."

Syria's President
BASHAR AL-ASSAD
Photo credit: Reese Erlich

four

Syria's President Bashar al-Assad: State Sponsor of Terrorism?

SYRIAN POLITICS are a lot like Syrian driving. You head at maximum speed toward your destination. If anyone gets in the way, you curse and honk your horn. If several drivers all head toward the same spot, you accelerate until the last possible moment, at which point you arrive first or slam on your brakes to let the other person pass.

Political power is exercised the same way. Syria has been on a confrontational road with the United States and Israel for many years. The government of President Bashar al-Assad seemed on the brink of collapse after being accused of assassinating former Lebanese prime minister Rafik Hariri in 2005. But it drove ahead at breakneck speed, swerved at the last minute, brought its troops home from Lebanon, and avoided a potential wreck.

Syria has also been willing to drive alongside America at times. In 1990 it sided with the United States during the first Gulf War, which was waged against a common enemy, Saddam Hussein. After the September 11, 2001, attacks, Syria shared intelligence with the United States about Islamic fundamentalists and helped thwart attacks on U.S. facilities. The Bush administration never acknowledged the assistance and later denounced Syria as a junior partner in the Axis of Evil. It sought to overthrow al-Assad's government.[1] But al-Assad resumed driving full-speed ahead and managed to stay on the highway long after President Bush pulled into the wrecking yard.

Despite many years of confrontation, President al-Assad and his government remain a mystery to most Americans. Successive U.S. administrations have sought to isolate Syria, accusing it of sponsoring terrorist organizations such as Hamas and Hezbollah. Yet al-Assad remains firmly in control of his country and will likely continue in power for some time.

In 2009, the Obama administration shifted course on Syria, sending several high-level delegations to meet with al-Assad. The post of U.S. ambassador had been vacant since 2005, but Obama appointed a new ambassador in 2010. The United States continues to impose economic sanctions against Syria even while it tries to negotiate détente. Once again, the United States labels a country as a state sponsor of terrorism only to lay the groundwork for a possible reversal. This time the change is based on a new U.S. administration in power, not any different policies by the supposed terrorist state.[2]

I have reported from Syria four times and interviewed President al-Assad twice. We talked about U.S.-Syrian relations, democratic rights within Syria, and, of course, terrorism. I wanted to unravel the mystery surrounding the president. I hope to offer a more realistic assessment of what he believes and what danger, if any, his government poses to people in the United States. And, believe me, it's complicated.

BASHAR AL-ASSAD wasn't supposed to be president. His father, Air Force General Hafez al-Assad, came to power in a coup in 1970. Hafez was grooming his other son, Basil, to lead the country. I was always fascinated by the photos and posters of Basil plastered along highways. He could easily be mistaken for a young Ringo Starr. Meanwhile, Bashar had become an ophthalmologist, graduating from the College of Medicine at the University of Damascus. He was taking speciality training in London when Basil died in a 1994 car crash. The president recalled Bashar to Damascus and trained him as his successor. Hafez al-Assad died in June 2000, and Bashar soon took over.

An official car drives me up to a hillside palace high above smoggy Damascus. As a security measure, cell phone coverage drops out partway up the hill. The palace is a very impressive place. After entering, I walk down about eight miles of red carpet to a set of huge wooden doors. And then, down at the end of the hall, a rather large man emerges out of a very small room. It's the president of Syria. Bashar al-Assad stands six foot two and looks thin and a little gangly. Born in 1965, he's still relatively young for a world leader. He has a firm handshake and speaks good English. I've had the opportunity to interview presidents and prime ministers from a number of different countries, and they were all stiff and formal. Al-Assad is genuinely friendly and immediately puts visitors at ease.

Al-Assad explains that he, like his father, believes in pan-Arabism, a nationalist ideology that held sway in the Arab world in the 1950s and '60s. Pan-Arabists believe in the unity of all Arab peoples and oppose imperialism. They are secular and very much oppose those who seize power in the name of Islam, such as the Taliban or al Qaeda. Al-Assad has a direct interest in avoiding sectarian war because his family is Alawite, a small Shiite sect that would certainly lose out if Syria fractured along religious lines.

Muslim fundamentalist groups have tried to overthrow the Syrian government in the past. In 1979 one such group attacked the military barracks in the city of Aleppo, killing 84 cadets and soldiers. In 1980 the Muslim Brotherhood, the country's main fundamentalist group, tried to assassinate Hafez al-Assad. In 1982 the Brotherhood led an insurrection in the city of Hama. The elder al-Assad bombed the city from the air and crushed the Brotherhood. During the 2000s fundamentalist groups have carried out sporadic terrorist bombings in Syria.

Al-Assad, noting his government's opposition to fundamentalist groups, bristles when the United States calls Syria a state sponsor of terrorism. He notes that the United States gave financial support to Osama bin Laden and the fundamentalist mujahedeen during the Soviet occupation of Afghanistan in the 1980s. "Syria has always opposed terrorists when the United States called them freedom fighters," he tells me.[3] Al-Assad says al Qaeda–style fundamentalism poses a real threat to Syria and the entire region. That's why after the September 11, 2001, attacks, Syria provided intelligence about such groups to the Bush administration. According to Seymour Hersh in the *New Yorker*, Syrian intelligence helped thwart a plan by al Qaeda to fly a hand glider loaded with explosives into the U.S. Navy's Fifth Fleet headquarters in Bahrain.[4] Al-Assad says, "We succeeded in preventing more than seven plots made by al Qaeda against the United States." In Bahrain there was going to be "an attack similar to the [USS] *Cole*."[5] He wouldn't go into more detail about the U.S.-Syrian cooperation.

But one case became quite public. On September 26, 2002, U.S. officials arrested Maher Arar, a Canadian citizen of Syrian origin. Based on false information from Canadian authorities, the United States suspected Arar of being a terrorist, held him for two weeks, and then secretly deported him to Syria against his will. Arar said he was tortured during his one year in Syria.[6] His is one of the few thoroughly documented cases of extraordinary rendition, in which the United States kidnaps and allows for the torture of suspected terrorists. A Canadian Commission of Inquiry later found that Arar had no connection to terrorism, and the Canadian government awarded him $11.5 million in compensation.[7]

U.S.-Syrian relations declined further after the March 2003 invasion of Iraq, which Syria strongly opposed. According to al-Assad, all intelligence cooperation between the United States and Syria ended in March 2005. By that time, the Bush administration was advocating regime change in Syria. "They tried to overthrow me," he says.[8] Successive U.S. administrations have accused Syria of aiding terrorism long before the rise of Osama bin Laden. In fact, Syria has been on the State Department's list of state sponsors of terrorism since 1979, the longest of any nation. According to the State Department, "President Bashar al-Assad continued to express public support for Palestinian terrorist groups. Hamas politburo head and defacto leader Khaled Meshal and his deputies continued to reside in Syria. Syria provided a safe haven for Meshal and security escorts for his motorcades."[9]

Does Syria's relationship with Hamas make it a supporter of terrorism? To answer this question, we need to look at some recent history. In the 1970s, Syria under Hafez al-Assad sought to lead the Palestinian movement, backing a number of Palestinian groups favorable to its views. Syria was part of the rejectionist forces who opposed partial peace treaties with Israel, including the 1978 Camp David Accords with Egypt and the Oslo Accords of 1993.[10] During the 1970s and '80s Syria supported rejectionist Palestinian groups such as the Popular Front for Liberation of Palestine, a small party that still has offices in Damascus. Syria strongly criticized PLO leader Yasser Arafat for being too moderate and in 1983 even tried to remove him from PLO leadership by backing insurgent leader Abu Musa. The effort failed and ended up alienating many Palestinians.

By the 1990s, however, the Palestinian movement had shifted radically. Leftist parties had lost support, with Hamas gaining popularity. The Islamist parties shared a common rejectionist stand with Syria in that era. Today, Bashar al-Assad's government allows Hamas and a smaller fundamentalist group, Islamic Jihad, to maintain offices in Damascus. Al-Assad tells me that of the ten Palestinian groups operating in Syria, those two are the most restricted. They are prohibited from organizing among Palestinians living in Syria, he says. "Hamas is the same as the Muslim Brotherhood," says al-Assad. "We don't allow their political activity. They can only make press statements. They are not allowed to give orders to followers in Palestine. We can't expel them to Palestine" because the Israelis would jail or kill them.[11]

Based on my interviews with ordinary people in the Palestinian areas of Damascus and with Hamas leaders, I think al-Assad's statements are only partially true. Syria and Hamas certainly don't agree ideologically, and Syrian officials would prefer that pro-Syrian, secular Palestinian groups had more popular support. But they don't. Hamas offers militant opposition to Israel, which is convenient for Syria at the moment. It's no secret in Damascus that Hamas leader Khaled Meshal meets with foreign leaders and directs Hamas's political activity. Numerous press reports indicate that he provides military leadership as well.

Al-Assad rejects the terrorism label for Hamas, as does most of the Arab world. He sees Hamas as part of a national liberation movement that has used violent tactics. In recent years, Syria has softened its rejectionist stance. Al-Assad tells me he's willing to accept an independent Palestinian state living in peace with an Israeli state so long as Israel returns all of the Golan and meets other international demands. Al-Assad sees the core of the problem as Israeli occupation of Palestinian and Syrian land, not terrorist tactics used by the Palestinians. Such tactics will stop, he says, when everyone reaches a political settlement. "The most important thing is our occupied land, the Golan," says al-Assad. "The United States should take into consideration that we see everything in Syria through our occupied land."[12] To understand this passionate feeling about the Golan, it's worth visiting the town of Quneitra.

⬛▬⬛▬

QUNEITRA, NEAR THE ISRAELI BORDER, was seized by Israel along with the rest of the Golan Heights during the 1967 war. In 1974

Israel agreed to a partial withdrawal from the Golan. Quneitra was to be returned as part of the armistice agreement. When the city was returned to Syrian control, however, it was totally destroyed. Syria and Israel blame each other for the devastation. The Israeli government argues that the city had been shelled during the 1973 Yom Kippur War. Any further damage was caused by artillery duels carried out by Syrian and Israeli troops over the intervening several years.[13] The Syrian government argues that, although there was some artillery damage, the Israeli forces intentionally flattened much of the city using bulldozers.

Today, Quneitra looks much as it did in 1974. A hospital and an Orthodox church are still standing. Without doors or windows, the hollow building shells are silhouetted against a brooding sky. Almost all the other buildings are destroyed in a distinct way: the roofs are intact and the structures have collapsed like pancakes. As we pull up in front of a block of pancaked houses, Syrian government spokesman Mohammad Ali says, "The bulldozer pushes or pulls a corner of the building. So the roofs collapse down. There is not any sign of bombardment at all. All the destruction was made after the Israelis decided to withdraw."[14]

British journalists who had visited the city just before and after the 1974 Israeli handover confirm the Syrian version of events.[15] A special UN Commission found Israel in the wrong, and the UN General Assembly called on Israel to compensate Syria for the intentional damage.[16] Israeli officials have criticized Syria for not rebuilding Quneitra. They ask what purpose is served by keeping the city deserted. Ali responds. "First, we want to keep it as a live witness of Israeli crimes. Secondly, Israeli forces surround the city from three sides. So it is unsafe for civilians to come back." The Syrian government has periodically asked former residents to gather deeds and other documents in anticipation of a possible return to Quneitra.

But it now appears that resettling the city must await a wider resolution of the Golan issue.

With U.S. sponsorship, Syria and Israel tried to reach a permanent peace settlement back in 2000. The Israelis were willing to give back substantial portions of the Golan, but insisted on maintaining a military presence on Syrian land—a deal breaker for then president Hafez al-Assad. In 2008 and early 2009, Bashar al-Assad and Israeli prime minister Ehud Olmert held indirect talks using Turkish officials as intermediaries. But talks broke off as it became obvious that ultraconservative Benyamin Netanyahu would be elected prime minister. Based on my talks with al-Assad and other Syrian officials, I'm convinced that if Israel returned all of the Golan and recognized an independent Palestinian state, Syria would work with Hamas and other Palestinian groups based in Damascus to accept a compromise, two-state solution. Rather than seek such a solution, the Bush administration further antagonized Syria by opening a new front in the propaganda war. Syria, the United States claimed, was intentionally allowing terrorists to cross its border to kill Americans in Iraq.

THE U.S. OCCUPATION OF IRAQ was a disaster almost from the beginning. Within months of the March 2003 invasion, guerrilla insurgents of various stripes began to fight what they saw as foreign occupation. Former members of Saddam Hussein's Baathist Party, Shia Muslim fundamentalists aligned with Iran, and a new group of Sunni fundamentalists calling themselves al Qaeda in Iraq all took up arms.[17] Al-Assad argues that U.S. military activities in Iraq have backfired, actually helping recruit young Muslims to the fundamentalist cause. "Extremism has increased in the region since the Iraq war," he says. "Youth need jobs. In the past most jobs came from the government. Now the United States is pushing private sector jobs. [Arab] society is becoming more closed, less liberal. We are going more to the right culturally and politically. This is our challenge. We must help our young people to be free thinkers.

"No military power in the world, even the United States, can control a small country militarily," al-Assad tells me. "You're going to have resistance, and you will not control anything . . . A full withdrawal is the only solution. Let Iraqis run their own affairs." Such a position sounded quite radical to American ears at the time of our 2006 interview, but by the end of 2008, the Bush administration had agreed to just such a plan. Under the Status of Forces Agreement (SOFA) signed by the United States and Iraq, the United States must close all its military bases and withdraw all troops by December 31, 2011.[18] But before the SOFA was signed, the Bush administration scapegoated Syria in an effort to explain the mounting American and Iraqi deaths.

The Bush administration accused Syria of sponsoring Baathist and al Qaeda insurgents. When the State Department listed Syria as a state sponsor of terrorism, it wrote, "Syria remained a key hub for foreign fighters en route to Iraq." The report further alleged that "members of the Abu Ghadiya network" operating in Syria "orchestrated the flow of terrorists, weapons, and money from Syria to al-Qa'ida in Iraq."[19]

On October 26, 2008, just days before the U.S. presidential election, the Bush administration sent four helicopters and dozens of special ops troops into Syria to capture or kill Abu Ghadiya. The ensuring disaster illustrates not only the false information the United States spreads about Syria but also what's wrong with U.S. military policy in the entire region.

PETER COYOTE AND I drive out to al-Sukariya, the town closest to where the raid took place. We rent a car with a driver, a young unshaven man named Qassem, who drives a dented vehicle of a curious purple shade. Speaking virtually no English except yes and no, Qassem is in need of diversion and slips a DVD into the front-mounted player of his car. He watches the Arab equivalent of MTV videos while driving 75 miles per hour. Occasionally, he takes his eyes off the undulating women dancers and the suave, mustachioed men to swerve away from oncoming Mercedes trucks.

The road to al-Sukariya is spare and beautiful. A lone shepherd minds dozens of sheep, who nibble at the sparse growth. Such nomads have wandered this area for centuries, passing through these expanses long before the Great Powers demarcated them as Iraq and Syria. Local tribesmen recognized no borders then, and the 375-mile-long border remains just as meaningless today.

Back in Damascus I ask President al-Assad if he's doing enough to protect the border from infiltrators. "Syria has better border control than other countries," such as Jordan or Iran, he says. "The United States can't control its border with Mexico, so how can Syria control its border with Iraq?"[20] While true, al-Assad's answer is not complete. Early in the war, Syrian troops did little to patrol the border, knowing some foreign fighters were slipping across. But even U.S. General David Patraeus admitted Syria had begun to more vigorously stop infiltration.[21] That's why the raid on al-Sukariya was so unexpected.

Peter and I drive to the outskirts of the city of al-Sukariya, where financially well-off Syrians build farms. They are usually summer houses with small vegetable gardens or fruit trees surrounded by high concrete block walls. We pull up to one such farm-to-be under construction. A 10-foot-high rectangle of walls encloses an area of hard-packed earth perhaps 30 by 80 yards. The night watchman unlocks the chain fastening the iron gate and swings it open. The unused hinges shriek.

After interviewing all the eyewitnesses and survivors of the al-Sukariya raid, we are able to piece together what happened that fateful day. A construction crew has been busy digging trenches and laying part of the foundation for the farm house. At dusk the helicopters come in, machine guns blazing and punching holes in the iron gate and concrete wall facing the Euphrates River. The machine guns and assault rifles fire so rapidly that the muzzle flashes appear to be shooting flames. Two helicopters land inside the walls. Dirt is blowing everywhere as soldiers leap from the bellies of the aircraft. The soldiers quickly kill the construction workers and a visiting neighbor with 8 to 15 shots each. Suad al-Khalf, the night watchman's wife and one of two adult survivors, stays inside the tent and clutches her son, Hassan. "No one fired back because no one had weapons," she says.

A soldier comes into the tent carrying an assault rifle. He looks at al-Khalf and Hassan, and walks out. Another soldier comes in a few moments later. He makes a gesture with his hand, palm down. She knows it means "do not move," and she does not. But then the big man with the gun frightens Hassan, who runs out of the tent. Without thinking she follows him outside. It is then that they shoot her, and she falls to the ground like the others lying along the walls. Hassan sees the red stains on the men's now tattered clothing. He turns and sees his mother, too, lying by the tent. But she is still moving. She is breathing, but she does not answer him as he calls her name. The blood frightens him. He is crying and calling. Within 15 minutes of their landing, the helicopters and soldiers leave. There is no one to help Hassan.

Two farmers who live nearby run to the farm, the first outside witnesses on the scene. They see six dead men, a dead teenage boy, and the seriously wounded Suad al-Khalf. "I recognized them," farmer Muhammad al-Abed tells us. "All of them were workers here. I knew the father personally, but also knew other members of his family." The patched tent is empty save for one small plastic sandal abandoned on the bare earth floor. Hassan stands over his mother. He says, "There were many soldiers." Asked if he knows where his father is, he replies, "He passed away. The Americans shot him."[22]

Anonymous Pentagon sources later claimed that the United States killed Abu Ghadiya, but never offered proof or even a detailed version of events. Once again the U.S. military botched a raid and then covered it up. Similar incidents, and others with unmanned drones, take place in Afghanistan and Pakistan. Because no high-ranking Democrats or disaffected Republicans raised questions about the al-Sukariya attack, it quickly faded from the news. So goes the War on Terror.

SYRIA IS INVOLVED in another controversy, this one of its own making. In 1975, Lebanon erupted in civil war as pro-Israeli, Christian Phalangists fought with Shia Muslim parties and the PLO, among others. In 1976, the Arab League asked Syria to head a peacekeeping force to end the civil war. Syria sent in troops and eventually crushed the right-wing Christian militias, although the war didn't formally end until 1990. Israel invaded Lebanon in 1978 and then again in 1982, occupying a 20-mile strip along the country's southern border. In 1982 the occupation gave rise to a new movement among fundamentalist Shiites called Hezbollah (Party of God). Iran's Revolutionary Guards helped organize Hezbollah, and the group initially called for making Lebanon into an Islamic Republic.

Ideologically, Hezbollah and Syria had little in common. But Syria allied with Hezbollah because of its growing popularity as a militant fighting force against Israel. Syria eventually cut deals with some Christian and other parties in Lebanon to create a pro-Syrian coalition. Syrian troops remained in Lebanon long after the end of the civil war, becoming the decisive political and economic power-broker. Lebanese businessmen provided key investments in Syria, and remittances by some 800,000 Syrian laborers in Lebanon help sustain Syria's economy.

Many Lebanese came to resent the seemingly permanent presence of Syrian troops and intelligence agencies. Syria argued that the

Arab League had sanctioned its intervention and that it remained in order to maintain stability. However, as Syrian opposition leader Sheik Nawaf al-Bashir tells me, "If there is a sick man, the doctor comes to treat him. Does that mean the doctor will live with him in the same house?"[23]

For their part, the United States and Israel regularly criticized Syria's presence in Lebanon. Both countries cultivated alliances with conservative Lebanese parties. The crisis came to a head on February 14, 2005. A motorcade carrying former Lebanese prime minister Rafik Hariri, who once supported Syria and later joined the U.S. camp, was driving down the coastal road in Beirut. A massive, remote-controlled bomb planted under the road killed him and 22 others. The United States, Israel, and other Western countries immediately blamed Syria. They argued that Hariri had angered Bashar al-Assad's government by calling for the removal of Syrian troops. Syria denied all responsibility for the bombing and said various Lebanese political and business interests had reason to kill him.

The pro-U.S. factions in Lebanon took full advantage of the anger generated by the Hariri murder. Mass demonstrations broke out, and by April Syrian troops were forced to withdraw, shaking al-Assad's government to its core. But Syria had a few cards left to play. It continued to ally with not only Hezbollah but other moderate Shia groups and Christian parties as well. Syrian troops withdrew, but its intelligence agents remained. Syria also maintained strong ties to the Lebanese military. Although the pro-Syrian parties lost the June 2009 parliamentary elections, they retained enough popular strength to block the pro-U.S. alliance from going after Syria or Hezbollah.

Meanwhile, the United Nations took up an investigation of the Hariri case. The first UN investigator, Detlev Mehlis, accused high-level Syrian officials of involvement in the assassination. But two subsequent investigators didn't repeat those charges.[24] In April 2009, a special UN tribunal created for the case released four Lebanese generals with Syrian ties who had been initially arrested for the bombing.[25] As of this writing, the investigation continues.

So, here we have it. Someone carried out a horrific terrorist bombing in broad daylight in the heart of Beirut. But as terrorists throughout history have discovered, assassinations don't necessarily lead to political change. In fact, such tactics can have results opposite from those intended by the perpetrators. The Hariri assassination ended up benefiting conservative, pro-U.S. allies in Lebanon. But because both the pro- and anti-U.S. coalitions continue to have considerable popular support, the political turmoil in Lebanon shows no signs of abating. As a practical matter, the Hariri investigation remains heavily politicized. If the United States deems Syria a potential partner in the Middle East, don't expect Syrian officials to be placed in the dock. But if Syria remains outside the U.S. sphere of influence, the indictment of top Syrian leaders remains a possibility.

FOR YEARS SYRIA HAS ALLIED ITSELF politically, militarily, and economically with Iran. Iranian leaders govern a fundamentalist, Shia Islamic state; Syria is a secular dictatorship that suppresses its Sunni Muslim fundamentalists. The two ruling elites have little in common ideologically. But the alliance has been forged for 30 years based on very practical considerations, beginning after Saddam Hussein attacked Iran in 1980. Syria and Iraq had long been enemies, dating back to a split in the Baathist Party that operated in both countries. So Syria sided with Iran during its bloody, eight-year war with Iraq. Iran provides oil, manufactured goods, and investments to Syria. The two countries support Hezbollah in Lebanon, and Iran ships money and arms through Syria into that country. In 2004 the two countries signed a mutual defense agreement.

For years, the United States has tried to split Syria off from Iran, emphasizing the ideological differences and hoping to encourage a pragmatic shift in Syria. After all, Hafez al-Assad abandoned his alliance with the Soviet Union when he supported the first Gulf War in 1990.[26] But breaking the Syria-Iran alliance won't be easy. From Bashar al-Assad's perspective, the United States has tried to overthrow both his and Iran's governments. And both the Bush and Obama administrations have threatened to bomb Iranian nuclear facilities.

President al-Assad strongly opposes such an attack. "If you do a military strike, you will have chaos. It's very dangerous. You can't resolve any problem in Palestine, Iraq, or Lebanon without Iran. The interest of the region and of the United States and the rest of the world is not to do such a thing, because the whole world would pay a very expensive price."[27] He also opposes economic sanctions against Iran as counterproductive. "From the experience in Iraq, and many different countries, sanctions won't do anything. But the consequences of destabilizing the region, by sanctions, by military actions, by any kind of means, will lead to destabilizing the whole Middle East."

It was clear to me that as long as the United States continues to demonize and threaten Iran, Syria will not break its alliance. If Israel and Syria were to reach a peace settlement and the West stopped threatening Iran, Syria would then not feel compelled to ally so closely with Iran.

So far we've only discussed Syria's foreign policy. What about President al-Assad's rule over his own people?

AS AUTHORITARIAN GOVERNMENTS GO, Syria is relatively benign. Iraq's Saddam Hussein tolerated no political dissent, jailing and viciously torturing anyone considered a threat. In Syria, soldiers don't stand on street corners, nor are there other outward signs of repression. Foreign newspapers are available, as is Internet access. But that doesn't mean Syria has a free press, the right to freely assemble, or other civil liberties. You don't want to get on the wrong side of Bashar al-Assad, that's for sure.

Syria has been ruled under a formal state of emergency since 1963 when the Baath Party seized power. According to a Human Rights Watch Report, "The Syrian authorities have maintained a tight lid on any form of criticism . . . The coming to power of Bashar al-Assad in 2000 carried with it hopes of increased tolerance for criticism, but these hopes ended abruptly a year later when Syrian authorities cracked down on a nascent civil society movement."[28] Amnesty International reports that Syria holds hundreds of political prisoners without trial and that some are tortured. Some Syrians who post blogs critical of the government have received three-month jail sentences.[29]

The Syrian government argues that most dissidents are fundamentalists, members of groups such as the Muslim Brotherhood. Fundamentalist groups have bombed the main Syrian intelligence agency and even attacked the U.S. Embassy in Damascus. But Syria also uses the threat of fundamentalism as an excuse to persecute people demanding any kind of change. I've met many Syrian critics who certainly weren't tools of the Muslim Brotherhood.

On one trip, I visited northern Syria, near the Iraqi border. After a bumpy car ride in the desert outside the eastern city of Der Ezzor, the estate of Sheik Nawaf al-Bashir rises in the distance. It includes a large house, a huge meeting hall, and a mosque. The sheik is the elected head of one of Syria's largest tribes. He's also a former communist and leading opponent of the government.

In May 2006, Sheik Nawaf was among 274 Lebanese and Syrian intellectuals who signed the controversial Beirut-Damascus Declaration criticizing the Syrian government's policies in Lebanon. The government arrested 13 of the signers. Sheik Nawaf was interrogated but not arrested. "We were questioned because in the declaration there were sections critical of the Syrian government. The police said it was wrong for us to call for establishing borders with Lebanon at this time. They warned me not to make the assassination of former Lebanese prime minister Hariri into an international issue."

Syria and Lebanon did not have full diplomatic relations at the time. Their border remained undefined, in part because of inequalities inherited from the border imposed by France during its colonial rule from 1920 to 1946. The Syrian government strongly criticized the Beirut-Damascus Declaration. As in similar claims over the years, it argued that dissenters were cooperating with the United States and Israel to destabilize the government. "It was written by a group in Lebanon who invited the United States to occupy Syria," President al-Assad tells me. "This was made in cooperation with them. This is treason. By Syrian law, they should go to court."[30] A number of the signers were tried and sentenced to jail terms. Two years later, Syria changed course and exchanged ambassadors with Lebanon. It also agreed to demarcate their border. The position advocated by the signers of the declaration was apparently two years ahead of its time.

As this case shows, Syria is a long way from extending democratic rights to its citizens. President al-Assad argues that one-party rule suits the conditions in his country. In 2006, he told me the government was beginning a dialogue among intellectuals and leading personalities to expand democratic rights in Syria. "It takes about a year of dialogue to define the frame that you are going to put the dialogue in. And after the dialogue, we decide. So it's going to be a national dialogue, it's not a dialogue inside the government."

Three years later, the dialogue, if it's taking place at all, has had no results. Syria remains a one-party state with few civil liberties. If Syria were in the pro-U.S. camp, the United States would overlook the repression and consider the government a bulwark against extremism. The governments of Saudi Arabia, Kuwait, and Egypt, for example, are far more repressive than Syria. But their regimes remain pro-American and therefore not on the list of state sponsors of terrorism. Such hypocrisy, however, doesn't excuse the lack of democratic rights in Syria.

According to all Syrian dissidents I've interviewed over the years, even if free and fair elections somehow materialized in Syria tomorrow, the new government would not suddenly find itself agreeing to U.S. policy. Syrians are united in opposing the Iraq War, demanding the return of the Golan, and supporting an end to Israel's occupation of Palestine. And they certainly don't want political change imposed by the United States. "We want peaceful change, without any war," says Sheik Nawaf. "We don't want to depend on foreign forces. Reform must come from inside Syria. We can compete with the Baath Party if given a fair chance. We don't want the government to fall; we want it to change from internal pressure. Let's learn the lessons from Iraq. We don't want chaos."

So, in calling for "democracy" in Syria, U.S. leaders should be careful what they wish for.

BASHAR AL-ASSAD is a complicated figure on the world stage. Although his country is weak economically and militarily, he holds veto power over negotiations with Israel. The Bush administration tried to remove him from power, but it didn't work. He runs an authoritarian regime that both represses his own people and prevents the growth of fundamentalist movements. Syria is one of the more peaceful and stable countries in a region fraught with strife and violence.

Syria's military and political support to Hamas and Hezbollah does not make it a state sponsor of terrorism. Although those groups have used terrorist tactics against civilians, Arabs and much of the third world consider them national liberation movements opposing imperialism. Nor does Syria present a threat to people in the United States.

Even if you consider Hamas and Hezbollah to be terrorists, Syrian support is very selective. A background report written by the centrist Council on Foreign Relations explains, "Syria has not been directly involved in terrorist operations since 1986, according to the State Department, and the country bars Syria-based groups from launching attacks from Syria or targeting Westerners."[31]

After one of my interviews with a high-ranking Syrian leader, the official car driving me home careened through the streets of Damascus. The driver looked at me strangely as I put on my seatbelt. Perhaps he thought I didn't trust his driving? Only later did I discover why he had the quizzical look. The seat belt hadn't been used in so long that the accumulated dust made a perfect diagonal stripe across my shirt. I looked like some kind of Middle Eastern crossing guard.

Cars and politics may be old and dusty in Syria, but Syrians follow certain predictable rules. American leaders should learn them. One of those rules should be not to assassinate people falsely accused of terrorism. To explore that, we'll go to the next chapter and meet Lebanon's Grand Ayatollah Fadlallah.

Grand Ayatollah
MOHAMMAD FADLALLAH
of Lebanon
Photo credit: Reese Erlich

five

Lebanon's Grand Ayatollah Mohammad Fadlallah: CIA Victim

ON MARCH 8, 1985, a man slowly drove a car packed with explosives along a West Beirut street and parked a few yards away from a five-story apartment building. Women and children were exiting Friday prayers at a nearby mosque. Minutes later the car bomb exploded with the force of 440 pounds of dynamite. It nearly leveled the apartment complex and two nearby seven-story buildings. Lebanese militiamen fired AK-47 rounds into the air to clear the streets and allow ambulances to pass. Hospitals quickly filled with the dead and dying. The bombers murdered at least 80 people that day and injured over 200. It was the largest bombing in Lebanon since the attack on the U.S. Marine barracks in 1983.[1]

But this was no terrorist bombing targeting Westerners. It was a U.S.-sponsored assassination attempt against Ayatollah Mohammad Fadlallah, whom the United States considered a leader of Hezbollah (Party of God). He escaped unharmed. According to Bob Woodward in his book *Veil,* then CIA director William Casey planned the car bombing because he thought Fadlallah had masterminded the Marine barracks attack. Casey paid $3 million to high-ranking Saudi officials to hire a hit squad.[2] Fadlallah tells me he finds Woodward's account credible.[3] After the horrific attack, Fadlallah's followers hung a huge banner over the ruins reading, "Made in the USA."

While most Americans think of themselves as victims of terrorism, people in the Middle East see themselves as victims of U.S. terrorist attacks. The U.S. government kidnaps and tortures suspected terrorists as part of its "extraordinary rendition" program. It detains and tortures civilians in Afghanistan and Iraq. People in the Middle East consider U.S. bombing raids that kill large numbers of civilians as a form of state-sponsored terrorism. Fadlallah himself faced several more assassination attempts after the 1985 bombing. In 1989, another car bomb packed with 220 pounds of explosives was parked on a road he normally took to Friday prayers, but security guards disarmed it.[4]

Fadlallah was never the devil portrayed by the CIA. He denies having planned the Marines bombing, and his subsequent actions lend credibility to the claim. During the Lebanese civil war of 1975–90, he opposed seizing American hostages and actually worked to get them freed. Since the end of that war, Fadlallah has emerged as a highly respected cleric with ties to Hezbollah but also with a fierce independent streak. Today Lebanese know him as much for his fatwas (religious rulings), such as opposing smoking and favoring women's rights, as for his ties to Hezbollah. Walid Jumblatt, a Lebanese parliament member strongly opposed to Hezbollah, tells me, "Sometimes Fadlallah sides with Hezbollah, sometimes not. Fadlallah has his own independent way of thinking. He always challenged the Iranian leadership in spiritual issues."[5]

Just as the United States once mischaracterized Fadlallah as a terrorist leader, so it distorts the history and views of Hezbollah. The group is certainly no Boy Scout troop. Hezbollah has used violence, espoused reactionary views, and imposed fundamentalist interpretations of Islam in areas it controls. But lumping it with al Qaeda as a terrorist group is factually wrong and politically dangerous.

FADLALLAH WAS BORN in Najaf, Iraq, in 1935 to Lebanese parents. He studied Islamic sciences and was soon to become an imam. He moved to Lebanon in 1966 and emerged as an activist cleric. Fadlallah became known both for his religious teachings and for establishing schools, a public library, a clinic, and a women's cultural center. He became an early supporter of Iran's Ayatollah Ruhollah Khomeini and subscribed to his theory that clerics should play a leading role in the government of an Islamic state.[6] After the 1979 revolution in Iran overthrew the dictatorial shah, the new clerical government sought to spread its version of Islamic revolution to nearby countries. Lebanon, with a 40 percent Shia Muslim population, became a prime target.

In 1975 Lebanon descended into civil war. Pro-U.S. Christian Phalangists and their allies fought Lebanese Muslims, the Palestine Liberation Organization (PLO), and their allies. Then Israel invaded Lebanon in 1982 with the intention of crushing the PLO. Amal, the main Shia party at the time, was seen as corrupt and unwilling to fight Israel. Several Shia militias, including dissident Amal members, came together to secretly form Hezbollah in 1982. Iran's Revolutionary Guard helped fund and train the new group, and Hezbollah became a strong defender of the Iranian Revolution.

Hezbollah adopted a right-wing, fundamentalist ideology and called for Lebanon to become an Islamic state ruled under strict Sharia (religious) law. From the beginning, it had sharp differences with the Sunni fundamentalist mujahedeen then fighting in Afghanistan against the USSR. The mujahedeen would eventually spawn Osama bin Laden and al Qaeda, who call for a Sunni Islamic empire to be created throughout the Muslim world. For bin Laden, Shiites are not even real Muslims. The antagonism between these different groups is longstanding.[7]

In 1985 Hezbollah laid out its strategy for making Islamic revolution. It saw the United States, Israel, and Lebanon's right-wing Christian Phalangists as the enemy. Like Iran, Hezbollah rejected both Western capitalism and Soviet communism. It charted a third path that sought to combine anti-imperialism with a strict interpretation of Islam. Hezbollah's 1985 program reads, "We call upon all of them [the Lebanese] to pick the option of Islamic government which, alone, is capable of guaranteeing justice and liberty for all. Only an Islamic regime can stop any further tentative attempts of imperialistic infiltration into our country."[8]

Like many young and militant revolutionary groups, the early Hezbollah disdained political compromise and deal making within the parliamentary system. The program says, "We could not care less about the creation of this or that governmental coalition or about the participation of this or that political personality in some ministerial post, which is but a part of this unjust regime." After the Israeli invasion, Hezbollah emerged as an effective guerrilla movement that sometimes used terrorist tactics. Fadlallah's religious teachings inspired Hezbollah, as did his emphasis on providing social welfare. Hezbollah established schools and hospitals that provided high-quality service at low cost. It also became the first Islamic group in recent times to use suicide bombers.

In April 1983 a car bomb blew up the U.S. Embassy in Beirut, killing 63 people, including eight CIA employees. In October, suicide truck bombers blew up American and French military barracks, killing 299 soldiers from both countries.[9] A little-known group called Islamic Jihad claimed credit. Some experts believe the bombings were executed by agents working with Iranian Revolutionary Guards and Syrian intelligence.[10] The United States and Israel blamed Hezbollah. Robert Baer, a CIA field officer who investigated the bombing, says the CIA was never able to determine who planned the attacks (see Foreword). U.S. officials later accused Hezbollah of kidnapping Americans living in Lebanon, assassinating CIA agents, and bombing a Buenos Aires Jewish community center.[11] Hezbollah vehemently denies these accusations but was clearly involved in violent activity aimed at driving both the United States and Israel out of Lebanon.

For their part, Hezbollah leaders accuse the United States and Israel of using terrorist tactics against them. In July 1989, Israeli soldiers kidnapped Hezbollah leader Sheik Abdul Obeid; in 1992 Israeli helicopters killed another leader, Abbas al-Musawi, and his wife and son. In February 2008, a car bomb killed Hezbollah leader Imad Mughmieh in Damascus, and Syrian authorities held Israel responsible.

In 1990 the various warring Lebanese factions ended the civil war. Two years later, with the strong encouragement of Syria, Hezbollah ran candidates in parliamentary elections, won eight seats, and became part of the largest bloc in parliament. This proved to be a turning point for the group. Hezbollah published a new parliamentary program that dropped references to creating an Islamic state. It developed an elaborate, aboveground political apparatus, including radio and TV stations. It even created a video game called Special Force, in which participants wage war against Israel. Hezbollah had not softened its stand against Israel, but it emerged as a respected and legitimate Lebanese political party.

IN THE SUMMER OF 1998, I visited a Hezbollah-controlled area in southern Lebanon. In theory the central government operates throughout the country. In reality, Hezbollah, and to a lesser extent Amal, controls the south and parts of Beirut. Lebanon's main north-south highway meanders through seaside villages and rolling hills. Wealthy vacation homes overlook impoverished towns. Giant posters of Amal leaders slowly give way to huge billboards with the wizened visages of Ayatollah Khomeini and Hezbollah leader Hassan Nasrallah. That's how each group marks the beginning of its territory.

You can learn a lot about a Muslim country by how women are dressed. Contrary to the image of women covered head-to-toe in Afghan-style burkas, most Muslim countries have evolved their own versions of the hijab, or covering. As residents in a relatively prosperous country, Lebanese women in cities often wear stylish, matching combinations of skirt, jacket, and headscarf. In the countryside, the women dress far more conservatively, sometimes wearing the all-black chador.[12]

In the 1980s, Hezbollah had required head scarves, prohibited alcohol, and even banned loud music in the areas under its control.[13] By the late 1990s, Hezbollah had changed policies, and women were free to wear a hijab or not. "We don't force anyone to follow Islam," Sheik Nabil Kaouk tells me. He was head of Hezbollah's military operations in south Lebanon. "We're not forcing anyone to wear the head scarf or not to drink. We do not agree with the Taliban in Afghanistan, for example. They have stopped people from watching TV and don't allow women to work. That's against Islam."[14]

However, in small villages, Hezbollah pursues a different strategy. It implements a process of "Islamization"—the inculcation of conservative moral and religious values. Farmer and Hezbollah member Ali Hammad Salman says that in his village, several residents used to sell alcohol, but Hezbollah closed their shops. "Since Hezbollah came to this village, they stopped people drinking," says Salman.[15]

Hezbollah runs an elaborate network of social welfare institutions, such as schools and hospitals, clearly designed to win support from the poor Shia residents of Lebanon. Within a decade of my trip, Hezbollah had developed a virtual parallel government with 4 hospitals, 12 clinics, 12 schools, and 2 agricultural centers.[16] After each Israeli military assault on civilian homes, Hezbollah officials arrive the next day to evaluate the damage and pay compensation. By the 1990s two Hezbollahs had emerged, according to Farid el Khazen, a political studies professor at the American University of Beirut. He tells me that Hezbollah maintains its military wing but that "Hezbollah has evolved from a clandestine group involved in acts of terrorism and kidnapping in the mid-80s to a full-fledged party. Today it has gained its own place on the Lebanese political scene."[17]

Hezbollah went on to win major victories as both a military and political force. In 2000, after 22 years of occupying part of southern Lebanon, Israel withdrew its troops. Hezbollah's deadly guerrilla war

made the occupation politically too costly for Israel. Hezbollah is credited throughout the Muslim world for having been the only Arab force
in history to defeat the Israelis. After that pullout, Hezbollah ceased
suicide bombings. Its leaders also sharply condemned the 9/11 attacks
on the World Trade Center in New York. Sheik Nasrallah says, "What
do the people who worked in those two towers, along with thousands
of employees, women and men, have to do with war that is taking place
in the Middle East? Or the war that Mr. George Bush may wage on
people in the Islamic world? Therefore we condemned this act—and
any similar act we condemn."[18] Nasrallah doesn't condemn the 9/11
attack on the Pentagon, however, because that was a military target.
"I said nothing about the Pentagon, meaning we remain silent. We
neither favored nor opposed that act," he says.

U.S. OFFICIALS UNDERSTAND that Hezbollah doesn't currently carry
out terrorist attacks on Westerners or Lebanese civilians. But the
United States continues to consider Hezbollah a terrorist organization because of its fight with Israel. Over the years, Hezbollah has
periodically fired missiles and artillery shells across Israel's northern border, although such attacks stopped after the 2006 war. Is the
United States right in its characterization of Hezbollah? Let's look at
both Hezbollah's ideological and practical view of Israel. Hezbollah
has always refused to recognize Israel as a legitimate state. Although
he does not speak on behalf of Hezbollah, Ayatollah Fadlallah
explains the viewpoint they share in common.

Fadlallah considers the early Zionist settlement of Israel as an
example of British colonialism importing a settler group onto Palestinian land. "Who made Palestine a sacred land for the Jews?" he
asks me. "God has not given them any document of ownership. We
don't understand why they should dislocate the Arabs living there."
He calls for a one-state solution, in which all Palestinians living in
exile would have the right to return to live anywhere in Israel, Gaza,

or the West Bank. "I don't accept Israel as a purely Jewish country because I believe that all the Palestinians living outside have the right of return. Why should Jews all over the world come to Palestine but not have the right of Palestinians to return?"

He insists that he is anti-Zionist, not anti-Jewish. "We have no theological problem with the Jews. Our problem with Israelis is political." Yet his one-state plan would only allow Jews to remain if they were born in Palestine before 1948. "We call for a society inhabited by the Jews who lived in Palestine before 1948 to live side by side with Christians and Muslims," he says. Fadlallah's position harks back to the earliest positions taken by Arab leaders, a view long rejected by the majority of Palestinians. Such a solution is highly offensive to Israelis because it ignores Israel's existence for over 50 years. The position also provides fodder for right-wing Israelis who say all Arabs want to expel the Jews and therefore no peace agreement is possible. In contrast to the Hezbollah position, all the major Palestinian groups have officially agreed to a two-state solution, in which Israel and Palestine would live peacefully side by side. Even Hamas signed the accord.[19]

In recent years Hezbollah leaders have in practice modified their stand. They now say Palestinians must decide this question for themselves. "At the end, this is primarily a Palestinian matter," says Sheik Nasrallah. "I, like any other person, may consider what is happening to be right or wrong . . . I may have a different assessment, but at the end of the road no one can go to war on behalf of the Palestinians."[20]

Why has the issue of Israel caused so much anger and passion in Lebanon? To find an answer, I visited Khiam Prison near the Lebanese-Israeli border in 2003.

I ONCE AGAIN DROVE to southern Lebanon, all the way to the Israeli border. The low Lebanese hills provide a scenic view of Israel's fertile fields below. Khiam, a former French military barracks, sits on a windswept hill. Israel used it as a prison from 1985 to 2000. I met former prisoner Mohammad Nayef, who was 14 when he was arrested at his house in 1994 and accused of being a member of Hezbollah. Israeli officers operated the prison and oversaw prison guards from the South Lebanon Army (SLA), a Lebanese militia created by Israel. Nayef was brought shackled and hooded before Israeli interrogators. He and others were forced to stay for four hours on their knees. They were beaten. Others were subjected to whippings and electric shocks.

A few days later, when the interrogators still hadn't gotten any answers, they brought in Nayef's sister and beat her in a nearby room. After that, "Of course I confessed," he tells me.[21] The Israelis wanted to get information about Hezbollah activities but also wanted to recruit spies and collaborators. They would then use such collaborators to extract more information after the torture sessions. Some of the SLA members and collaborators stayed in Lebanon and at least one lived near Nayef. "I can't forgive these collaborators, and we don't talk to them." But he abides by Hezbollah's orders not to harass or injure the former collaborators. Nayef was never charged with a crime, let alone put on trial. He was released when Israel abandoned the prison as part of its withdrawal from Lebanon in 2000.

Israeli officials argue that the prison was run by the SLA and that Israel can't be held responsible for the mistreatment. However, Nayef and numerous other Lebanese witnesses say Israeli officers in the prison fully participated in the abuses. Amnesty International reported numerous similar stories from other Khiam prisoners.[22] From 2000 to 2006 Hezbollah kept Khiam intact as a living museum. During the 2006 invasion of Lebanon, however, Israeli jets bombed and destroyed the site.

FOR MANY YEARS Hezbollah's official position was that it would disarm if Israel withdrew from Lebanon. After the 2000 Israeli withdrawal, the United Nations certified that Israel had left all Lebanese territory. Hezbollah refused to disarm, however, arguing that Israel continues to occupy Shebaa Farms, a 10-square-mile strip of land Israel seized from Syria in the 1967 war. Syria now agrees that Shebaa is Lebanese territory, so Hezbollah's argument has some validity. In reality, however, Hezbollah kept its arms for future wars with Israel and to give it power in internal Lebanese political battles. It would soon be tested in both.

In July 2006 Hezbollah guerrillas launched a raid into northern Israel and 10 Israeli soldiers died in the fighting. In the wake of that incident, Israel invaded Lebanon in an effort to crush Hezbollah. After inflicting horrific damage on the country, it withdrew its forces, leaving Hezbollah's organization still intact.[23] The Lebanese considered the war a defeat for Israel, and Hezbollah's popular support skyrocketed. Support cut across religious lines. According to a Beirut Center opinion poll, 87 percent of Lebanese supported Hezbollah's resistance against Israel, including 80 percent of Christians.[24]

But popularity can be fleeting in Lebanon, as evidenced by incidents even prior to the 2006 Israeli invasion. After former prime minister Rafik Hariri was assassinated, Hezbollah's ally Syria was accused of the bombing. The assassination sparked massive demonstrations against continued Syrian troop presence in Lebanon, and Syria was forced to withdraw in April 2005. Several Christian and moderate Muslim parties formed an anti-Hezbollah, anti-Syria coalition and hoped to gain control of parliament. Hezbollah and its allies, including Sunni Muslims and a conservative Christian party, fought back with mass demonstrations of their own. From 2006 to 2008, the two opposing camps called for mass demonstrations and set up tents in Beirut's downtown. Violence broke out between the warring factions, and Hezbollah used arms domestically for the first time since the end of the civil war.

The anti-Syria coalition, with strong backing from the United

States, accused Hezbollah of breaking its promise not to use arms against fellow Lebanese. They claim Hezbollah is the only armed group in Lebanon, but that's not accurate. Every major political group in Lebanon is armed. In 2008 I visited the summer home of a major politician opposed to Hezbollah. A spare bedroom held AK-47s and rocket launchers, backup for the family guards in case of new armed conflict. When the 2008 fighting broke out, Walid Jumblatt's Druze forces fought back with arms. "The other groups were armed," he admits. "But Hezbollah took over Beirut in a couple of hours." Hezbollah simply has the largest and best organized of the armed factions in Lebanon.

Hezbollah did cross a line by using arms domestically. But so far, it hasn't had much political impact. The Lebanese Army won't take on Hezbollah because doing so could precipitate another civil war. As Jumblatt tells me, "It's just impossible to disarm Hezbollah militarily. We have to wait until the regional and internal conditions are such that they themselves agree to become part of the Lebanese Army."

In the June 2009 parliamentary elections, the pro-U.S. coalition won 71 of 128 seats, the remaining 57 seats going to Hezbollah and its allies. Hezbollah received 13 seats, a loss of one from the previous elections. By December, the ruling coalition had to relent, however, and the prime minister paid a respectful visit to Syria and expressed willingness to compromise with Hezbollah.

Then Hezbollah got hit with an unexpected scandal. In September 2009, Lebanese businessman Salah Ezzedine was arrested for perpetrating a massive fraud. Leveraging his close ties to Hezbollah and other Shia leaders, he ran an investment scheme that reportedly promised 40 percent profits.[25] When his empire collapsed in bankruptcy, he was called the "Bernie Madoff of Lebanon." Hezbollah leaders denied any connection with Ezzedine's scheme, but several top ranking members were reportedly defrauded.[26]

Hezbollah, it seems, has come full circle. In the 1980s it was a militant and violent opponent of imperialism, disdaining compromise and calling for an Islamic state. By the 1990s it had developed a significant parliamentary base. And by the 2000s it had its own financial scandal. Hezbollah has certainly evolved, and so has Ayatollah Fadlallah. I finally got a chance to meet him at the end of 2008 after arriving from Damascus.

THE MOUNTAINS SEPARATING SYRIA AND LEBANON are strikingly different. The Syrian side is brown, dry, and arid; the Lebanese side is plump with chocolate-colored earth and swollen with moisture. Green is everywhere in Lebanon, and the overall impression is as lush and wealthy as Syria is dry and poor. Peter Coyote and I are being driven from Damascus to the ancient city of Baalbek in Lebanon. For years, the citizens here have elected Hezbollah to run the city and represent them in the national parliament.

On this day Hezbollah is planning a large rally to protest Israeli actions in Gaza. Crowds are massing as we try to find a way through the jam-packed avenues. The local government has closed many streets as a security measure to protect high-ranking Hezbollah leaders who are arriving for the demonstration. As we thread our way out of Baalbek, the streets fill with thousands of Hezbollah supporters chanting pro-Palestinian slogans, waving fists, and banging drums.

We later drive to Beirut for our meeting with Fadlallah. We travel at high speed in a two-car caravan around the city's periphery, arriving in predominantly Shiite west Beirut. The neighborhood makes a stark contrast to the affluent Christian sections of east Beirut. Tiny shops edge the road. Cars and scooters in various states of disrepair choke the sidewalks. Knots of men talking in small groups clog the way as our cars twist through narrow, unmarked streets. We stop in front of the thickest steel gate we've ever seen—nine inches at least, if not a foot. It slides back on oiled rollers, allowing us to enter a small, sheltered driveway flanked by armed guards. We are escorted into a building with a bare lobby lit by a fluorescent tube. Security men make a barrier at one end, and their chief, a large man with a head that looks like it could break rocks, regards us with undisguised hostility. His minions search us with the same standards of thoroughness as Hamas did, but with even more disdain.

Once again cell phones and fountain pens are dismantled. My shoulder bag full of recording equipment is confiscated; after much argument, it is inspected and returned. Security check over, we are led into a long, undecorated, and narrow room lined with plush chairs. Several unidentified men sit along the walls, and others enter with a professional HD video camera and tripod. They arrange microphones and lay cables for their own taping of the meeting. Apparently, they are as interested in filming a film star as we are in recording an ayatollah. Fadlallah enters wearing dark brown robes and the black turban of a sayyid, a direct descendant of the prophet Mohammad. At 73 years old, his hair and beard are silver-gray, and shadows form large crescents under his eyes. His wears dark raiments and a worn visage. He appraises us carefully.

Western governments and media have often called him the "spiritual advisor" to Hezbollah, but he denies this role. Indeed, Hezbollah always considered Iran's Ayatollah Ruhollah Khomeini as its spiritual leader.[27] Speaking calmly in response to our questions, he says that today, while he enjoys "good relations" with Hezbollah, he also is on good terms with other Shia and Sunni parties. He plays a role similar to Iraq's Ayatollah Ali al-Sistani, a respected cleric who receives support from various Shia parties and factions.

A former secretary general of Hezbollah, Subhi Tufeili, says Fadlallah was never a Hezbollah leader and always sought to be a spiritual influence for all Shia Muslim groups. "We can say that he [Fadlallah] was consulted on most major political issues, and that he was a cardinal stopping point for us . . . Even I tried on several occasions to suggest . . . that he should have a larger role or a specific position within the group, but the sayyid preferred not to. He wanted to be [there] for everyone."

Fadlallah seeks to distinguish his views from those of the Sunni-based al Qaeda and similar jihadist groups. "I was the first Islamic cleric to denounce the September 11 events," he says. "Our religion does not permit the punishment of innocent people. Islam is against terrorism in all forms." Although other clerics denounced the attack before he did, Fadlallah did indeed strongly oppose the terrorist act on both moral and political grounds. "Beside the fact that they are forbidden by Islam, these acts do not serve those who carried them out but their victims, who will reap the sympathy of the whole world . . . Islamists who live according to the human values of Islam could not commit such crimes."[28]

But what about the killing of Israeli civilians, always a more contentious issue in the Arab world? He calibrates his answer carefully. He says Muslims should never intentionally target civilians, but sometimes civilians die in the course of a war of liberation. He reminds us that "when Europe fought the Nazis, there were a lot of civilian casualties." We note to ourselves that he doesn't criticize either Hezbollah or Hamas, who have at times intentionally targeted Israeli civilians. Collateral damage is often excused in wartime, unless you happen to be the collateral.

Fadlallah's and Hezbollah's views on resistance to Israel are widely shared in the Arab world, but ironically, his views about domestic policy are considered much more controversial. In recent years he has distanced himself from the Iranian theory that clerics should rule. He no longer believes Lebanon should become an Islamic state. His views on women are even more controversial. He writes that men and women should be treated as equals.[29] He issued a fatwa banning wife beating and giving women the right to defend themselves against such attacks. He tells me, "I've always believed that the woman is not less than the man in any aspect. I believe that women have the right to learn, to work, to practice politics, to elect and be elected, and assume political leadership." Like Christian and Jewish clerics who believe in a strict interpretation of their religions, Fadlallah opposes abortion rights for women. He makes an exception when the woman's life is in danger.

Perhaps most controversial in the context of the Middle East, Fadlallah issued a fatwa opposing smoking. I note that some men in the room are puffing up a storm. We inquire if his followers abide by the fatwas. "I banned smoking because it causes cancer," he says. "The minority accepted my fatwas but the majority did not." His men laugh nervously and stub out their butts.

We ask Fadlallah his opinion of U.S. policy and the prospects for peace. He says, "We do not have any problem with the American people. Our differences are with the American administration." Fadlallah expresses concern that President Obama will not break from past Mideast policy. "U.S. presidents talk about supporting democracy," he says, "but in the Middle East, and the third world in general, they support the worst and ugliest kind of dictators. In the 1940s, people in the region believed the United States was a country with principles. They preferred the United States over France, the old colonial power. We want the United States to go back to those principles."

It's hard to know if Fadlallah is merely spouting rhetoric or speaking sincerely. He has a long history of antagonism toward U.S. policy. Most U.S. leaders would probably disagree with his interpretation of what principles they should uphold. But today Fadlallah enjoys the respect of ordinary Muslims and virtually all the political factions in Lebanon. He acts as a mediator between those factions during times of civil turmoil. And he could do the same between the United States and Hezbollah if an American administration ever wakes up to the need for basic change in U.S. policy. Had the CIA succeeded in blowing up Fadlallah back in 1985, it would have killed a man who could help bring peace to the region.

MOHSEN SAZEGARA,
a founder of Iran's Revolutionary Guard and
current activist against the government of Iran
Photo credit: Kaveh Kazemi, Hulton Archive, Getty Images

six

Mohsen Sazegara, Terrorist Governments, and Iran's Democracy Movement

I DRIVE THROUGH THE NOISY STREETS of central Tehran at two in the morning. It's just days before the Iranian presidential election of 2009. Thousands of people jam the streets, honking horns and shouting slogans. Most wear green armbands and support reformist candidate Mir Hussain Mousavi. Smaller numbers wave banners favoring incumbent President Mahmoud Ahmadinejad. Most of the Mousavi supporters are economically well off. They drive new cars and wear designer sunglasses. Who else wears sunglasses at night? The young men wear polo shirts with designer labels. Many of the women have all but abandoned the hijab, wearing scarves barely covering their hair.[1]

I covered elections and opposition activities in Iran during three previous trips. But the 2009 elections are different. This time people seize the streets of Tehran and shout reformist slogans in defiance of the government, thinking the authorities are not likely to crack down during the election campaign. Indeed, police give up trying to control the crowd that night and simply tell people to move along. Tens of millions of Iranians go to bed on Friday, June 12, convinced that either Mousavi won the election outright or that he would face a runoff with Ahmadinejad. Some even stay up all night. Others wake up Saturday morning to learn that the official vote count shows Ahmadinejad won 62 percent of the vote. They are stunned. "It was a coup d'état," more than one friend tells me. The anger cuts across class lines and goes well beyond Mousavi's core base of students, intellectuals, and the well-to-do.

Within two days, hundreds of thousands of people, perhaps as many as a million, demonstrate peacefully in the streets of Tehran and other major cities. Most do not call for a change in government, but they are angry at the vote fraud. Over the next few weeks, the mass movement evolves from protesting the elections to calling for much broader freedoms. I could see the changing composition of the marches. The upper-middle-class kids in tight jeans and designer shirts are there. But so are growing numbers of workers driving motor scooters, men in clerical robes, and women dressed conservatively in chadors. The city of over 8 million came alive as demonstrations spread from the relatively affluent north Tehran to the working class districts in the south of the city.

Thirty years of anger at injustice boil to the surface. Workers express resentment at the 30 percent annual inflation that robbed them of real wage increases in 2008.[2] Independent trade unionists call for decent wages and the right to organize. Some demonstrators want a more moderate Islamic government. Others advocate a separation of mosque and state, and a return to the parliamentary system they had before the 1953 coup. For the first time in memory, demonstrators publicly criticize the supreme religious leader, Ayatollah Ali Khamenei. Protestors unite in calling for greater democracy. I am a firsthand witness to the most significant political uprising in Iran since the 1979 revolution that overthrew the shah.[3]

Exiled opponents of the government rushed to support the mass movement. Among them was Mohsen Sazegara, a founder of the Iranian Revolutionary Guard and now a political activist living near Washington DC.

SAZEGARA IS A BUSY MAN. He has converted the basement in his suburban Virginia home into a multimedia center. He records videos for YouTube. He conducts interviews on the phone and over Skype. He dedicates all his time to getting rid of the current government in Iran. He has unique qualifications as a dissident. In 1979 Sazegara flew with Ruhollah Khomeini from Paris to Tehran, which began the ayatollah's triumphant ascension to power. Sazegara helped form the Iranian Revolutionary Guard Corps and later held sub-ministerial posts in the revolutionary government. He soured on the revolution, however, was jailed in the infamous Evin prison, and was eventually allowed to leave the country for medical treatment.

Recent U.S. administrations have labeled Iran as the world's "most active" state sponsor of terrorism because of its support for Hamas, Hezbollah, and other insurgent groups.[4] In 2007, the U.S. government labeled the Revolutionary Guard a terrorist organization. Sazegara agrees that the Revolutionary Guard is a terrorist organization today, but argues that it has changed over the years. It "was not a terrorist organization in the beginning. What we had in mind was a people's army to defend the country. We thought we might be attacked by the U.S., because the U.S. was the supporter of the shah."[5]

Sazegara has made a 180-degree turn since his days in the Revolutionary Guard. In Washington DC he took a job at a strongly pro-Israel think tank. In February 2010, he was appointed a "Visiting Fellow in Human Freedom," at the George W. Bush Presidential Center in Dallas. He speaks at forums organized by the right-wing American Enterprise Institute and is frequently quoted as an expert source in conservative publications. An article in the *Wall Street Journal* claims his house has become "the de facto U.S. headquarters of Iran's opposition,"[6] a designation that angers other Iranian activists who point out that no one in exile leads what has become known as the Green Movement. "He has no following in Iran," says Muhammad Sahimi, an Iran expert and professor at the University of Southern California.[7] "In my opinion he is nothing but a man who wants to ride the Green Movement wave to power."[8]

Sazegara rejects such criticisms, arguing that his YouTube videos and emails directly reach 100,000 Iranians. He claims 500,000 Iranians see his postings as they are passed around the Internet. He considers himself a secular democrat in the liberal tradition. He tells me that he makes no claims of leadership of the Green Movement. "I try to help people in Iran get acquainted with civil resistance and nonviolent activities."[9] Yet, neither does he object when conservative media proclaim him a major leader.

The controversy over Sazegara illustrates different trends within the movement. Some, such as Sazegara, see the U.S. government as an ally and favor strong sanctions against the Iranian regime; others do not. To better understand that contradiction, let's consider some recent Iranian history through Sazegara's eyes.

SAZEGARA WAS BORN on January 5, 1955, in Tehran. His father was a shopkeeper and his mother a housewife. At age 14 he started organizing against the shah's dictatorship. "When I was in the ninth grade, I was active in a massive demonstration against the increase of bus fares. I encouraged all my classmates not to go to classes." In the early 1970s he joined a Muslim student group at an engineering university. "We arranged several demonstrations. Some became very big; we were on strike and didn't take the exams, so the whole semester was cancelled."

Sazegara was heavily influenced by the sociologist and revolutionary thinker Ali Shariati, who combined elements of Marxism with calls for Shia Muslim activism into what he called "red Shiism." Sazegara tells me, "Every Muslim activist in those days was affected by his ideas." By the late 1970s, Sazegara had become a follower of Ayatollah Khomeini and lived in the leader's compound outside Paris. "We believed in a kind of Islamic utopia. We thought we are going to have a new type of civilization, a new kind of life for human beings."

Sazegara had developed some theoretical knowledge about guerrilla war. In France, he put the theory into practice. He trained volunteers from the United States, Europe, and Iran. "I taught the volunteers in just a one-week course how to keep secrecy, how to have relationships with other groups, and how to start your group in Iran." With the idea of forming a people's army, Sazegara says, those groups went to the Middle East to be trained in armed struggle. Radical Palestinian groups taught them in Lebanon, and the Syrian army trained them in Syria, he says.[10]

After Ayatollah Khomeini came to power, Sazegara became one of five provisional members of the board of commanders of the newly formed Revolutionary Guard. Khomeini and other revolutionaries didn't trust the Iranian army, fearing some officers didn't support the Islamic revolution. Even today, Sazegara defends the concept of creating a people's army to defend the revolution against all kinds of enemies. "We had the bitter experience of British and American conspiracy against the government of Mossadegh in 1953. In those days we were really afraid of a military coup d'état against the new regime."

But after three months he realized military life didn't suit him. He went on to head Iranian state radio, and later became deputy minister for heavy industry, and deputy chairman of the budget and planning department. By 1986 he became disillusioned with the Islamic Republic. Iran has a hybrid capitalist system with clerics and government officials controlling vast sectors of the economy.[11] He saw the system wasn't working. "We had to join the world, [and develop] some kind of market economy."

In 1986 he was falsely accused of involvement in the 1981 bombing that assassinated the country's president and prime minister. Sazegara was jailed in Evin, the prison infamous for holding political prisoners. He was ultimately jailed four different times and was incarcerated a total of 195 days.[12] "I witnessed scenes that I never imagined could happen: scuffles, use of abusive language, insults, people groaning and lamenting—although I didn't see them beating anyone. But I heard the voice of a girl telling an interrogator, 'I can't endure more torture.'"[13]

While Sazegara's early support for the Iranian Revolution could be considered radical, I don't think he was ever a terrorist. Today he opposes all violent revolution and believes that dictatorships inevitably result. "It does not matter who will be in power, if you establish a regime which is based on revolutionary ideology, there is no accountability for the leader, the head of the regime." In 2004 Sazegara was released from prison for the second time. Strange as it may seem, his Evin prison interrogator had given Sazegara his cell phone number. So when Sazegara's doctors recommended surgery abroad for heart and eye problems, Sazegara phoned the interrogator. "If I were you," Sazegara said, "I would let me out of Iran. If I come back I will be in your hands again." The interrogator checked with higher authorities and 43 days later, the government returned his passport and Sazegara left for London. He never did find out his interrogator's real name.

When Sazegara arrived in Washington after leaving Iran, the Bush administration neoconservatives were in power, and he eventually acculturated to the Washington climate. Sazegara took a job with the Washington Institute for Near East Policy—a hawkish, pro-Israel think tank formed by members of the American Israel Public Affairs Committee (AIPAC).[14] He became friends with neoconservative, American Enterprise Institute scholar Michael Rubin. Sazegara established his own nonprofit, the Research Institute for Contemporary Iran. But he really became well known after the rise of the Green Movement in 2009. Sazegara was surprised at how quickly the movement developed. "I was astonished like many others."

I REMEMBER QUITE WELL the day it all began. Within two hours of the polls closing on June 12, 2009, the government announced that President Ahmadinejad had won reelection with an overwhelming majority. But there were some glaring discrepancies. Ahmadinejad supposedly carried all the country's major cities, including Mousavi's hometown of Tabriz, where Mousavi had held massive campaign rallies. The other reformist candidate, Mehdi Karroubi, received 55 percent of the votes in his home province of Lorestan in 2005 but only 4.6 percent in 2009, according to official figures. For many Iranians, it just didn't make sense. This wasn't the first instance of vote fraud. When I covered the 2005 elections, Ahmadinejad barely edged out Karroubi in the first round of elections. At the time Karroubi raised substantive arguments that he was robbed of his place in the runoff due to vote manipulation. He wrote a letter to the Supreme Leader Khamenei calling the vote fraud "the blackest page in the history of ideological struggle in Iran." But under Iran's clerical system, there's no meaningful appeal.[15]

On the day of the 2009 election, election officials illegally barred many opposition observers from the polls. The opposition had planned to use SMS text messaging to communicate local vote tallies to a central location, but the government shut down all SMS messaging. So the vote count was entirely dependent on a government tally by officials sympathetic to the incumbent. I heard many anecdotal accounts of voting boxes arriving pre-stuffed and of more ballots being printed than were accounted for in the official registration numbers.

In the following months, firsthand accounts of vote fraud emerged. London's Channel 4 News interviewed a former Basij member who said militia members were ordered to cast votes for people in some areas. In areas with large numbers of students, the votes weren't counted at all. The Basij member said, "When the voting was over, the boxes were opened, but not all of them. A few were opened and counted. Then we received another order to send the boxes to the main centre."[16]

A study by professors at Chatham House in London and the Institute of Iranian Studies at University of St. Andrews, Scotland, took a close look at the official election results and found some major discrepancies. For Ahmadinejad to have sustained his massive victory in one-third of Iran's provinces, he would have had to carry all his supporters, all new voters, all voters previously voting centrist, and about 44 percent of previous reformist voters.[17]

Keep in mind that Ahmadinejad's victory took place in the context of a highly rigged system. The Guardian Council determines which candidates may run, based on their Islamic qualifications. As a result, no woman has ever been allowed to campaign for president, and sitting members of parliament were disqualified because they had somehow become un-Islamic. The constitution of Iran created an authoritarian theocracy in which various elements of the ruling elite could fight out their differences, sometimes through elections and parliamentary debate, sometimes through violent repression. But it has never been a democracy.

TWO DAYS AFTER THE ELECTION, the marches were small and scattered. But the spontaneous outburst grew. By Monday tens of thousands were marching in the streets of major cities. And by Tuesday perhaps a million marched silently, holding up signs reading "Where is my vote?" The Iranian government responded to these peaceful protests with savagery, killing at least 70 people.[18] An estimated 4,000 were held without charges or simply disappeared. But repression didn't kill the movement. On July 17, 2009, tens of thousands came to Friday prayers in support of the opposition. Instead of chanting "Death to America," they chanted "Death to the Dictator," a reference to Supreme Leader Ali Khamenei. Police attacked them with clubs and tear gas.

Back in 1999, when students protesting repression and demanding democracy flooded off the university campuses and into the streets, the government's repressive apparatus crushed the movement within a week. But in 2009–10, the movement showed amazing resiliency. In part, that's because Khamenei and Ahmadinejad had alienated previous supporters within the working class. Workers as varied as bus drivers and steel workers held sporadic protests over economic grievances and demanded independent unions. Workers were particularly angry because state-owned companies had failed to pay their wages for months at a time. Workers protested Ahmadinejad's plans to raise prices on subsidized food and gasoline, and to privatize state-owned industries. The Network of Iranian Labor Unions (NILU) wrote, "Ahmadinejad's price liberalization scheme is nothing but a regurgitated version of the infamous shock therapy treatment devised by the late Milton Friedman of the University of Chicago fame. It was first applied in Chile in the late 70's and later in East and Central Europe with devastating effect for the poor and working classes."[19]

Demonstrators mainly used word-of-mouth and phone calls to organize because the government had shut down text messaging and periodically disrupted Internet communications. Contrary to media myth in the West, this was not a "Twitter Revolution," a term that both mischaracterizes and trivializes the important mass movement.[20] The myth began when the Iranian government prohibited foreign reporters from traveling outside Tehran without special permission, and later confined us to our hotel rooms and offices. Eventually, almost no foreign reporters were allowed to stay in Iran. CNN, BBC, and other cable networks were particularly desperate to find ways to show the large demonstrations and government repression. So they turned to social networking sites such as Facebook and Twitter in a frantic effort to get information. Because reporters were getting most of their information from Tweets and YouTube video clips, the notion of a "Twitter Revolution" was born. We reporters love a catch phrase and, Twitter being all aflutter in the West, it seemed to catch on, even if it was highly misleading.

The majority of Iranians have no access to Twitter. While reporting in Tehran, I didn't encounter anyone who used it regularly. A relatively small number of young, well-off Iranians do use Twitter; a much greater number have access to the Internet, including many in rural areas. However, in the beginning, most demonstrations were organized through word-of-mouth, mobile phone calls, and text messaging. Somehow, however, "Text Messaging Revolution" doesn't have that modern, sexy ring tone. Later, the government blocked many Web sites, monitored Facebook accounts, and slowed Internet speeds to make audio and video access difficult. By focusing on the latest in Internet communications, U.S. media characterize a genuine mass movement as something supported mainly by the "Twittering Classes." In fact, the Green Movement has become multigenerational and multiclass—not dependent on any particular form of technology.

IN THE MONTHS FOLLOWING the 2009 elections, the Iranian government launched its worst repression in 20 years. It arrested or exiled virtually every major opposition leader with the exception of Karroubi and Mousavi. Nobel Prize–winner Shirin Ebadi was living in exile, so the government arrested her apolitical sister, Noushin Ebadi, in an effort to pressure the outspoken human rights activist. Noushin had a heart attack in jail and was later released. Opposition Web sites and foreign press documented numerous cases of abuse, torture, and rape in government prisons.[21] The movement quickly became decentralized and morphed beyond the control of the reform leaders. One Mousavi aide said, "The movement has no head and it is he [Mousavi] who follows the people not the other way round."[22] Many of the decentralized demonstrations became more radical than anything envisioned by Karroubi or Mousavi.

On December 19, 2009, Grand Ayatollah Hossein Ali Montazeri died. He had been the chosen successor to Ayatollah Khomeini until he sharply criticized government policies and was eventually put under house detention. He had strongly supported the Green Movement, and during events mourning his death, thousands of people came out into the streets of Tehran, Isfahan, Tabriz, and other cities. His death coincided with the Shia celebration of Ashura, when, according to Shia Islam, the evil Caliph Yazd murdered Hussein, grandson of the prophet Muhammad. As Professor William Beeman, chair of the Anthropology Department at the University of Minnesota, wrote, "Now the public is equating opposition candidate Meir Hussein Mousavi with Imam Hossein. They chant 'Ya Hossein, Ya Mir-Hossein' in their opposition marches. Ayatollah Khamenei is now equated directly with the Caliph Yazd in street slogans and banners."[23]

That's the equivalent of American protesters comparing former president Bush to Pontius Pilate, which, after some reflection, isn't a bad idea.

On February 11, 2010, the Green Movement attempted to reprise those tactics, hoping to infiltrate pro-government demonstrations being held to commemorate the 31st anniversary of the Iranian Revolution. Some Iranians in exile hyped the upcoming protests as a decisive battle to end the regime. But the government bussed in tens of thousands of supporters to give a show of support, while it brutally repressed anyone suspected of being a Green protestor. Only hundreds of antigovernment demonstrators appeared, and many activists began to re-evaluate their tactics.

Mohsen Sazegara came in for particular criticism for being out of touch with conditions inside Iran. He had exaggerated the power of the movement in his Internet video messages to Iran, according to critics. The *New York Time* wrote that he had predicted the demonstrations "would change the balance of power and pave the way for a 'final action' against the government . . ."[24]

TO UNDERSTAND THE MOVEMENT in Iran, let's engage in some informed speculation about recent U.S. history. Imagine for a moment that you're living in Florida in 2000 right after the November presidential election. Democrats accuse George W. Bush of having stolen the election from Al Gore. When the U.S. Supreme Court issues its famous 5–4 ruling stopping the recount and giving the election to Bush, instead of quietly accepting the verdict, Al Gore calls the decision illegitimate and advocates mass demonstrations. You, along with hundreds of thousands of angry people, flood into the streets in peaceful marches. The police shoot into crowds, killing some and injuring many others. President Bush declares martial law to put down the insurrection, blaming al Qaeda and Iran for instigating the violence.

Al Gore and his Democratic Party advisors quickly lose control of the movement, in part because they had no intention of sparking a revolution, and in part because such mass uprisings always develop their own momentum. Some anti-Bush protestors want to reform the system and restore genuine constitutional rule. Others call for revolution, arguing that the constitution is inherently undemocratic (for example, the Electoral College allows for manipulation of the popular vote and corporate power really controls elections). The reform versus revolution debate shakes the country and starts to impact Republicans, independents, and even members of the ruling elite.

That's what happened in Iran.

NO ONE CAN ACCURATELY DEFINE the political goals of the Green Movement because they are diffuse and constantly evolving. Some activists favor revolution. They want to create a secular constitution guaranteeing human rights while continuing to oppose Western domination of their country. They express solidarity with people in Palestine and Lebanon, for example, without endorsing the government's support for Hezbollah and Hamas.

Others simply oppose anything the Islamic Republic favors. They argue that Iran should take care of its own problems before supporting Islamic struggles elsewhere. So they chant "Neither Gaza, nor Lebanon, my life is for Iran." Homayoun Poorzad, a leader of the Network of Iranian Unions, tells me some activists reject the government's "lifeless and awful propaganda. The result is that many people take the polar opposite position from the government."[25]

Yet another group wants to maintain the current constitution and the country's support for Islamic causes abroad. Presidential candidate Karroubi, for example, prefers the slogan, "Both Gaza and Lebanon, my life is for Iran." Karroubi says, "We do not want to make another revolution and do not seek to overthrow the regime." He goes on to say, "I accept the Islamic republic, and I accept the constitution. I don't agree with slogans that call for changing power structures."[26]

Five leading Iranian Islamic intellectuals living in exile issued a manifesto for the Green Movement that tries to bridge the gaps among the various tendencies. It calls for the resignation of Ahmadinejad, the freeing of all political prisoners, and freedom of press and political association. But it also makes more radical demands that contradict the current constitution, such as election of the supreme leader and judges, term limits on elected officials, and keeping security forces out of politics.[27] But people inside Iran have little ability to collectively discuss such demands, so it's hard to know how much popular support they have and if they could genuinely bridge the differences.

Iran remains a sharply divided country, with some Iranians continuing to support Khamenei, Ahmadinejad, and the Islamic Republic. The government is able to mobilize tens of thousands of supporters in demonstrations and at Friday prayer services.[28] In many cases the government packs the events with civil servants, poor workers promised food and money, and off-duty soldiers. But Ahmadinejad does appeal to the country's deeply religious population. And he wins some adherents by portraying himself as an economic populist and an anti-imperialist opponent of the United States and Israel.

THE SITUATION becomes even more complicated because some ethnic minorities resolutely oppose Ahmadinejad but don't support the Green Movement leaders. Nearly half the population of Iran is ethnic minorities, many concentrated along the country's borders. Voters in the southeast province of Baluchestan, for example, had a 14 percent lower voter turnout in 2009 than in 2005, indicating a lack of support for either side.[29] Green Movement candidates faced mixed results among other minorities as well.

On the last day of my 2009 trip to Iran, I had to exit the country quickly. My 10-day journalist visa was about to expire, and I didn't care to find out what would happen if I overstayed. My flight from Tehran to Erbil in northern Iraq had been cancelled at the last minute. So I flew into northwestern Iran and then took a bus to Iraq. That took me through the Kurdish region of Iran, an area normally off-limits to U.S. reporters.

The Kurdish region is noticeably poorer than other parts of the country. The tall buildings and wide freeways of major cities become two-lane roads and undeveloped farmland. We pass through villages where Kurdish houses are made from crumbling cement and old stones. Men wear the distinctive Kurdish baggy trousers, waist sash, and headdress. Everyone on the bus is Kurdish, and we have some revealing conversations. They oppose the repressive political and economic policies of Ahmadinejad. And the passengers particularly oppose the Iranian government's repression of the Kurdish language and culture. But as one man argues, the opposition candidates didn't say enough about Kurdish rights.

Underground Kurdish political parties have been organizing inside Iran for years, seeking greater democracy and federalism. The Komaleh and the Democratic Party of Iranian Kurdistan (PDKI), two of the main parties, called for a boycott of the elections. After June 12, they opposed the election fraud and the repression of the Green Movement. But they also opposed Mousavi, Karroubi, and the other reformist politicians who they say are trying to maintain the status quo.

Mostafa Hejri, head of the PDKI, lambasts the reformist leadership because "they hope to show that the Islamic Republic is a much better system than a secular, nonreligious form of government." He calls on Green Movement activists to broaden their support by allying with Kurds and other ethnic minorities. "People will only join this movement if there is a concrete plan for the realization of their violated rights and demands following the victory of this movement."[30]

Other groups felt more sympathy for the Green Movement leaders. The exiled Kurdish Democratic Party and all the above-ground Kurdish parties organizing inside Iran threw their support behind reformist candidates. But Kurds and other ethnic minorities living in the border provinces didn't demonstrate in large numbers to protest the election.[31]

ALTHOUGH IRANIANS ARE DIVIDED about the Green Movement, it has no lack of supporters abroad. Even U.S. conservatives were quick to claim paternity. Conservative radio host and columnist Larry Elder had the audacity to argue that the success of the Iraq War inspired Iranians to rise up against "Islamofascism," just as neoconservatives had predicted.[32] Mohsen Sazegara has been playing along with similar conservative misrepresentations for some time. At a forum sponsored by the American Enterprise Institute, he said, "Contrary to my generation which [was] anti-U.S., revolutionary, anti-imperialist as we called ourselves in those days, this new generation astonishingly is really pro-West and pro-U.S. especially. That is wonderful."[33]

The reality is far more complicated. When Sean Penn, Norman Solomon, and I covered the 2005 presidential elections, we interviewed many ordinary Iranians. People were very friendly toward us as Americans but very hostile to U.S. policy against their country. We visited Friday prayers where 10,000 people chanted, "Death to America." Afterward, some of those same people invited us home for lunch.[34]

A major Western public opinion poll conducted in Iran in September 2009 reflects that same reality. Iranians are friendly to the

West in the sense that 63 percent support having diplomatic relations with the United States. But a whopping 77 percent view the U.S. government unfavorably, with 71 percent expressing "not much confidence" in President Obama. According to the pollsters, "Iranians distrust American intentions when it comes to democracy promotion in the Islamic World. Only 16 percent believe the U.S. unconditionally supports democracy in Muslim countries."[35]

Some Iranians in exile, however, continue to see the U.S. government as an important ally. Sazegara, for example, tells me that former President Bush "supported the freedom and democracy struggle of Iran. As an Iranian, I agreed with his stands, not only him, but any government who supports the struggle."[36] Now that Obama is in power, Sazegara says he supports Obama's policies. Sazegara opposes U.S. or Israeli military attacks on Iran but believes the United States should tighten sanctions against the Revolutionary Guard and their business enterprises.

Many leading activists inside Iran sharply disagree. They point out that the United States has imposed economic sanctions against Iran since 1979 with little impact except to hurt ordinary people.[37] Mir Hussain Mousavi, for example, says additional sanctions "would impose further pain on a nation that has already suffered a great deal by its schizophrenic rulers."[38]

Similarly, Mohammad Ali Abtahi, a vice president under reformist president Khatami, tells me he opposes sanctions and U.S. intervention in the region.[39] I interviewed him in June 2009. In conversation with me and in previous interviews with others, Abtahi criticizes U.S. policy in Afghanistan and Iraq. He notes that the United States won some support in the region for ousting Saddam Hussein and the Taliban. But the United States remains as an occupying force in both countries. As a result, polices "which could have been an opportunity to defeat terrorism, led to an expansion of extremism."[40]

On June 16, 2009, only days after our interview, Abtahi was arrested by Iranian authorities and accused of having ties with counterrevolutionary groups, planning a so-called Velvet Revolution and other crimes. Under duress, he was forced to publicly confess to all the charges except one. "I think the capacity for such a thing [Velvet Revolution] exists in the country, but I don't know if there was a real intention to do it."[41]

And there's the crux. Tehran accuses Washington of fomenting a Velvet Revolution, and the United States wouldn't mind seeing one. But that's not what's actually happening.

The first Velvet Revolution overthrew the communist-led, pro-Soviet government in Czechoslovakia in 1989. Since then, the term has been used to describe mass movements that ousted governments in Georgia, the Ukraine, Serbia, and other countries. Western governments and media loudly trumpet them as popular uprisings because they always installed pro-U.S. regimes. In reality, the so-called revolutionaries created autocratic governments that benefited the wealthy at the expense of the poor. But because they were pro-American, all is forgiven.

Since 1979 every U.S. administration has sought to bring Iran back into the American sphere of influence as it was under the shah. The United States seeks control of Iran's oil, sea lanes, and potential military bases. U.S. efforts at regime change reached a peak under George W. Bush, when his administration actively sought to overthrow the Iranian government through Velvet Revolution, violent coup, and/or ethnic separatism. Bush funded American nonprofit groups and ethnic guerrillas that used terrorist tactics against Iranian authorities.[42] It carried out these activities in the name of fighting terrorism and stopping development of an Iranian nuclear bomb.

Both the Bush and Obama administrations argue that Iran's nuclear power program is a cover for building a bomb. However, the UN's International Atomic Energy Agency (IAEA) has never declared that Iran has a nuclear weapons program.[43] In a National Intelligence Estimate, the CIA and other U.S. intelligence agencies also concur that Iran doesn't have a current nuclear bomb program.[44]

Even if Iran were to enrich uranium to bomb-grade quality, it would take many years to have a functioning atomic weapon that could be used in war.[45] So, why the panic? The United States and Israel continue to use the nuclear issue to scare Americans and pressure Iran.

The Obama administration's approach to Iran is more sophisticated than its predecessor's. The administration emphasized diplomacy and sanctions, and downplayed military threats. But it hasn't substantially changed demands that it knows Iranian leaders will have a tough time meeting. It wants Iran to stop all aid to allied groups in Lebanon, Palestine, and Iraq. And Defense Secretary Robert Gates says that Iran must turn over uranium intended for use in generating electricity to Russia and France, because Iranians have done nothing "to stop their progress toward a nuclear weapon."[46] The United States and Europeans would never turn control of their low-level enriched uranium to third countries because it might jeopardize their ability to generate nuclear power. Why should Iran be any different?

For their part, Iranian leaders haven't exactly been interested in meaningful compromise. Former vice president Abtahi explains why Iran has rejected overtures from the United States. "It was important for Iran, which had a revolution and wanted to lead the Islamic world, to have a big and important enemy such as the United States. So that was precisely the reason many of the initiatives put forth to overcome the problems in relations between the two countries were always met by obstacles."

Debate within the U.S. government continues. Some officials want to emphasize a military attack, others want crippling sanctions. But they are united in pursuing the economic and military interests of the United States, not those of the people of Iran. U.S. officials claim to support the popular movement in Iran while the House and Senate prepare severe new sanctions that would sharply restrict gasoline exports to Iran and have a devastating impact on ordinary people.

Although Iran is a major producer of petroleum, it refines insufficient amounts of gasoline due to economic sanctions and its own economic errors.

Meanwhile, elite lobbying groups are trying to create the illusion of a popular movement favoring strict sanctions. In early 2010 a group called United Against Nuclear Iran forced Caterpillar Corp. to stop a subsidiary from selling construction machinery to Iran. United Against Nuclear Iran's leadership includes former CIA director James Woolsey and Mark Wallace, a former Bush administration diplomat.[47]

Sazegara's position on sanctions dovetails with such groups. He advocates strict sanctions against the Revolutionary Guard but admits the sanctions would also hurt ordinary Iranians. "Although it might be harmful for the life of the people, their lives are in danger from the Revolutionary Guard. It doesn't matter if there is some pressure on their life economically."[48]

That's more easily said sitting in Washington than facing hardships in Iran. Such sanctions backfire because people who perceive they are under siege from a foreign power rally round their government. I've met Iranian activists who want to see the United Nations and other multilateral bodies condemn Iran's human rights violations, and even put Ahmadinejad on trial for his crimes. But they make a sharp distinction between genuine international efforts and those pushed exclusively or mainly by the United States. The people of Iran are interested in neither military attacks nor crippling sanctions.

If the United States wants to genuinely support the people of Iran, it should simply allow the movement to follow its own course. Labor leader Poorzad tells me, "The best support Obama can give is no support. Even with human rights, we don't need it. It's not going to affect anything, other than give this regime a pretext."

And Iranians have good reason to fear U.S. support. Just look next door to Afghanistan.

MOHAMMAD NIZAMI,
former head of Afghanistan TV and Radio
under the Taliban
Photo credit: Reese Erlich

seven

Mohammad Nizami:
The Taliban's Golden Voice

MULLAH MOHAMMAD IS'HAQ NIZAMI looks a lot like Osama bin Laden. He's tall, thin, and sports a long black beard. He wears a carefully wrapped turban. Nizami even has the same habit of wiping his lips with his beard. When nervous about answering a question, he grabs a patch of beard and daintily wipes his lips as if brushing them with a fine linen napkin. And like bin Laden, he's been on the American bad guy list for years.

Nizami was once a top leader in the Taliban government in Afghanistan. He was a senior advisor and spokesman for Mullah Mohammad Omar, the one-eyed, onetime, clerical ruler. Nizami headed up the country's radio and TV network, and his golden-toned voice became known to Afghans through his daily radio commentaries. He fled into exile with the Taliban after the 2001 U.S. invasion and published its magazine *Shine* while living in Peshawar, Pakistan.

In 2007 he switched sides, and President Hamid Karzai welcomed him as an ally. Nizami has tried to broker a number of peace deals with his former Taliban comrades. Karzai government officials promote him as an example of how to win over former Taliban to participate in the democratic process. But after spending a long interview with Nizami and digging into his life story, I learned he hasn't changed much from the old days. Afghanistan has a long history of

leaders switching sides. Some of Karzai's cabinet ministers were generals during the Soviet occupation of 1979–89.[1] The staunchest U.S. ally
against the Soviet Union, Gulbuddin Hekmatyar, is today a wily and
effective guerrilla fighter *against* the United States. These transforma-
tions often take place without the leaders changing their basic views.

So it should come as no surprise that Nizami continues to favor an
Islamic government for Afghanistan ruled by strict Sharia (religious)
law. He opposes equal rights for women and wants to see foreign
troops withdraw. Only the timetable has changed. As a Taliban leader
he called for the immediate withdrawal of U.S. and other foreign
troops. Today he tells me, after "U.S. troops strengthen the Afghan
police and military, then they should leave. If day by day they support
Afghan military and day by day they decrease their numbers, this will
bring peace and benefit for all sides."[2]

That tolerance for the continued presence of U.S. troops is suffi-
cient to make him an ally in the view of the United States and Karzai.
The dirty secret of the Afghan war is that the Taliban's ideology and
political views on the future of Afghanistan are quite similar to many
of Karzai's top supporters, including members of his cabinet. They,
too, want a fundamentalist-ruled Afghanistan and have nothing but
contempt for democratic elections.[3] The war pits two sets of fundamentalists against one another. One side has U.S. support.

MOHAMMAD NIZAMI was born in 1960 in Nangarhar Province in eastern Afghanistan near the Pakistan border. "My mother was a housewife and my father was a religious teacher," he tells me. "I studied with
him, and I learned a lot from him." Nizami studied in the provincial
capital, Jalalabad, and later became a mullah himself. His education
was interrupted, however, by the Soviet invasion in December 1979.[4]

"I knew from the history of the Soviet Union that they would
want Afghanistan as their own state, and that they would want to

control Afghanistan forever. My reaction at the time was to start jihad, to take up arms against the Soviet Union." His family fled to Peshawar, where young Nizami joined the guerrilla group led by Gulbuddin Hekmatyar, the most right-wing, anti-communist, and fanatically religious of all the opposition groups. Nizami eventually took charge of the group's clandestine radio broadcasts.

Pakistan was crawling with opposition parties and militias. But both the CIA and Pakistani Inter-Services Intelligence (ISI) favored Hekmatyar. Nizami says that 50 percent of U.S. funding went to his group, with the remainder being split among the other opposition parties. Hekmatyar's group "was older and well organized," explains Nizami. "They had a strong structure and a big base of support in all of Afghanistan." But analysts say Hekmatyar actually lacked popular support and relied on Pakistani and U.S. aid to bolster his power. He quickly developed a reputation for corruption and barbarity, often spending more time attacking fellow mujahedeen than Soviet troops. The United States spent at least $600 million on Hekmatyar, according to author Peter Bergen. He wrote, "Hekmatyar's party had the dubious distinction of never winning a significant battle during the war, training a variety of militant Islamists from around the world, killing significant numbers of mujahedeen from other parties, and taking a virulently anti-Western line."[5]

The ISI and Saudi government leaders helped recruit foreign Muslims to fight in Afghanistan. Osama bin Laden was among them. As the son of one of the richest men in Saudi Arabia, bin Laden played an important role in financing and organizing the U.S.-backed mujahedeen. The seeds of today's al Qaeda and Taliban networks were planted during the Afghanistan-Soviet war, all nurtured with U.S. and Saudi funds. In those years, both Democratic and Republican administrations were focused on defeating the Soviet Union. Supporting right-wing Muslim fundamentalists was just one means to undermine the main enemy.

The United States government ignored the obvious, long-term problems of creating the mujahedeen movement. Jimmy Carter's national security advisor Zbigniew Brzezinski helped initiate the CIA's covert war. In 1998 he said, "That secret operation was an excellent idea . . . What is most important to the history of the world? The Taliban or the collapse of the Soviet Empire? Some stirred-up Muslims or the liberation of Central Europe and the end of the cold war?"[6]

The CIA trained these "freedom fighters" in skills that would come in quite handy in later attacks on U.S. targets. "The U.S. gave the mujahedeen brand-new and very sophisticated weapons," Nizami tells me. U.S. shoulder-fired rockets enabled them to shoot down Soviet helicopters and planes. The mujahedeen never shied away from using terrorist tactics. They targeted teachers, civilian officials, and anyone else perceived to be helping the pro-Soviet Afghan government. In those years, Nizami spent most of his time broadcasting propaganda from Peshawar. But in the summer, he'd return to his home village as a guerrilla fighter. "It was too hot in Peshawar," he says with the only flash of humor exhibited during our interview. "So I went to the mountains near my village to fight the Russians."

But the CIA was not only providing weapons and training. The United States needed an off-the-books method for financing the expensive mujahedeen effort. Afghanistan had been producing opium for centuries. Locals smoked or ate the opium, but before 1979, it hadn't been processed into heroin. The mujahedeen learned to make the narcotic, hoping to both finance the insurgency and turn Soviet soldiers into drug addicts. In 2002 I interviewed a former Pakistani drug smuggler and several high-level ISI officers. They explained that the United States shipped arms to the mujahedeen through the port of Karachi, trucked them overland to the Afghan border, and shipped them by mule into Afghanistan. The mujahedeen then used the same transport route in reverse to smuggle out heroin. Today, the highest concentrations of Pakistani drug addiction are along that trail. Shaukat Qadir, a retired Pakistani army brigadier general, tells me that the CIA instructed top generals in Pakistan's ISI to sanction the drug trade. General Qadir says that while the Drug Enforcement Agency (DEA) tried to stop the heroin smuggling, the CIA "as a matter of policy was saying it's okay." CIA officials justified drug dealing on the grounds they were promoting a greater good, according to Qadir, who bases his conclusions on conversations with fellow generals and top ISI officers.[7]

In 1989, the defeated Red Army withdrew from Afghanistan. The high cost of the war in money and lost lives contributed to the Soviet Union's implosion two years later. The war also cost 1 million Afghan lives; another 5 million became refugees in neighboring countries. Within a few years, the mujahedeen groups began fighting among themselves, destroying parts of Kabul and other major cities.

Meanwhile, the United States rewarded some of its allies. Sheik Omar Abdel Rahman is a blind Egyptian cleric who had worked with Osama bin Laden in Afghanistan in the 1980s. He was granted a U.S. visa in 1990 despite being on a State Department terrorist watch list. The Immigration and Naturalization Service even gave him a green card. Within a few years, he and others were convicted of masterminding the 1993 World Trade Center bombing, which killed 6 people and injured over 1,000. U.S.-supported terrorism was coming home.[8]

By 1994 Afghans had grown weary of the mujahedeen warlords constantly battling one another. Pakistan's ISI helped form the Taliban, which means "students." Taliban fighters included mujahedeen defectors, clerics, and Afghan students from madrassas in Pakistan. They promised strict Islamic rule to combat the mujahedeen chaos. By 1996, the Taliban controlled 90 percent of Afghanistan, all but a small northern section of the country.

The Taliban imposed one of the most rigid Sharia systems in the world. Mullah Omar banned elections and declared himself Amir, or commander, trying to recreate the structure of the old Muslim empires. Although he initially consulted with a *jirga*, or council, he increasingly ruled by decree. Provincial governors lacked formal education beyond religious schooling and were incompetent running the government. The officials applied a bizarre interpretation of Islam, banning TV, movies, music, chess, and even kite flying and raising pigeons. In 2001 the Taliban destroyed the centuries-old Buddhas carved into a mountainside in Bamyan Province because they were "idolatrous."

The Taliban ran a human rights–violating dictatorship that was out of touch with Afghan traditions. From the 1950s to '70s Afghanistan was no democracy, but a tolerant form of Islam held sway. Women's rights were respected somewhat. Under the Taliban, women were required to be covered head to toe in burkas. They were banned from attending school, working at most jobs, and they were allowed on the street only if accompanied by a close male relative. Men were punished for trimming their beards. Thieves had their hands amputated; adulterers were stoned to death in public events at the former soccer stadium in Kabul.

As head of the country's TV and radio network (Voice of Sharia), Nizami accepted and promoted the Taliban system. The Taliban interpreted Islam as prohibiting any representation of the human body, which meant that portraits, film, and TV were banned. Nizami's radio network was filled with political propaganda and religious exhortations. As chief spokesperson for the radio, he had a regular broadcast. Even today Afghans of that generation remember his voice. In my interview, Nizami says TV was also banned for political reasons. "The television was closed temporarily, not permanently, because the great Mullah Omar and other people around him decided to stop the television. Some people were using satellite dishes to receive foreign broadcasts. We were reaching the people by radio, and the people were getting our news."

Nizami became famous for one incident during his tenure. Other government officials wanted to destroy the national TV archive. Nizami refused. "This archive contained the history of Afghanistan," he tells me. "It was a national investment; it belonged to all Afghans."

THE U.S. GOVERNMENT initially gave tacit support to the Taliban, offering no public criticisms of its seizure of power in 1996. U.S. administrations frequently ignore human rights violations by a government that can provide stability and a favorable investment climate for U.S. corporations. At first, the Taliban appeared to fill the bill. In 1997 UNOCAL negotiated with Taliban leaders to build an 800-mile natural gas pipeline from Turkmenistan through Afghanistan to Pakistan. A Taliban delegation visited UNOCAL's headquarters in Sugarland, Texas. The company even arranged to train 140 Afghans as pipeline workers.[9] The U.S. government calculated that it could use the Taliban to circumvent Russian control of oil and gas coming from the Caspian Sea. The pipeline would also provide a tidy profit to a U.S. company. But the deal ultimately fell through due to political instability in Afghanistan.

U.S.-Afghan relations soured as the Taliban proved to be a destabilizing force. In 1998 the Taliban killed thousands of civilians in the city of Mazar-e-Sharif and murdered 10 Iranian diplomats at the local consulate. Iran massed 200,000 troops along the border but a possible war was averted. Later that year al Qaeda, based in Afghanistan, bombed U.S. embassies in Tanzania and Kenya, killing over 200 and wounding more than 4,000, mostly Africans. In retaliation the Clinton administration ordered a missile attack on an al Qaeda training camp in Afghanistan. But U.S. relations with the Taliban on some issues remained positive. In May 2001, just five months before the 9/11 attack on the Pentagon and the World Trade Center, Secretary of State Colin Powell announced plans to give the Taliban $43 million in humanitarian aid in recognition of its successful eradication of opium poppies.[10]

Osama bin Laden had taken up residence in Afghanistan and developed close ties with the Taliban. Just two days prior to the 9/11 attacks on the United States, al Qaeda agents assassinated Ahmad Shah Massoud, the most charismatic of the anti-Taliban leaders fighting in the northern part of the country. But Osama bin Laden says the Taliban had no advance knowledge of the 9/11 attack.[11] Indeed, at the time, the Taliban's foreign minister denounced it. Nizami explains to me that "we criticized it, and every Muslim should have criticized the attack." The Taliban offered to either put bin Laden on trial if the United States provided evidence or extradite him to an Islamic country for trial under Sharia law.[12] The Bush administration, already determined to invade, dismissed the offer out of hand. It demanded immediate extradition of bin Laden and other al Qaeda leaders, and the closing of all terrorist training camps, followed by direct U.S. inspection. The administration knew the Taliban wouldn't meet those demands. On October 7, 2001, the United States invaded.

Perhaps the Taliban was not serious about putting bin Laden on trial. After the United States requested his extradition in 1998, the Taliban said there wasn't enough evidence linking him to the African embassy bombings. But the Taliban was under tremendous international pressure after 9/11. What if the United States had seriously pursued the divisions between al Qaeda and the Taliban? If bin Laden had been put on trial in a third country, the world would be very different today. The United States insisted on invading less than one month after the attack. As we will see, the American Empire had much larger goals in Afghanistan than just punishing those responsible for 9/11.

I ARRIVED IN AFGHANISTAN in January 2002. I was writing, among other stories, about a Global Exchange delegation made up of relatives of 9/11 victims. They oppose the invasion and would provide an alternative view to the pro-war hysteria passing for news in much of the mainstream media. But due to a series of mix-ups, I arrive in Kabul with no fixer, someone to translate and arrange interviews, and no way of contacting Global Exchange. Landline phones are useless, and Afghanistan has no cell phone system. On the other hand, the country is crawling with reporters. They are to prove useful.

I grab a cab to the former Intercontinental Hotel where Global Exchange is supposed to be staying. The once opulent hotel sits on a hill overlooking bustling Kabul. By 2002 it's a wreck. It has no functioning phones, and reporters have to make international calls from a satellite phone in the lobby for seven dollars a minute. Electricity works sporadically, and no water flows above the fifth floor. In the dead of winter, the hotel has no heat. Did I mention the place is completely full? The hotel receptionist has no record of any of the Global Exchange people staying at his establishment.

Then an Afghan man named Umer approaches me in the lobby, asked if I was a journalist, and inquired if I needed a fixer. I am both thankful and suspicious. This guy could be anyone from a legitimate journalist to a Taliban spy. Without agreeing to pay a fee, I offer to try out his services. "Find me a room at the inn," I say, not knowing if he would get the biblical reference. "Hell, just find me an inn."

We careen through the chaos of Kabul in a hired taxi. U.S. soldiers mix with mujahedeen wearing the traditional *shalwar kameez*, or long shirt and loose pants, and turbans. They all have AK-47s slung over their shoulders. Not a single traffic light works. Driving etiquette consists of speeding through narrow streets at 40 miles an hour, honking the horn, and applying squealing brakes only as a last resort. Umer takes me to each of the hotels frequented by foreign journalists. All are half-star guest houses with intermittent electricity and bathrooms down the hall. I run into Peter Arnett, the former star reporter for AP, CNN, and NBC. He is staying at a dive considered quite good because the manager delivers two buckets of hot water to the room each morning, enough for an awkward shower. But that luxury accommodation is full.

Umer and I found a guest house farther downtown once used by Taliban officials visiting from the countryside. That means it lost another half star. The room features burn marks on the rug and a blown-out light socket on the wall. The room has one outstanding quality, however. It's available, so I grab it. The owner keeps an AK-47 leaning on a wall next to his bed. I never do find out if it was protection against insurgents or angry customers. Later I meet Dan Rather, then anchoring the CBS Evening News from Kabul. He had just interviewed some of the Global Exchange delegation members that morning. Through Rather I am able to find the guest house where they were staying.

The hassles we faced as foreigners paled by comparison to those faced by ordinary Afghans. The 1990s civil war had destroyed whole sections of Kabul, and most of it was never rebuilt. The U.S. air assault hit some housing and civilian infrastructure. The majority of Afghans live in poverty with no running water, paved roads, or access to medical care. Initially, many Afghans welcome the U.S. invasion. The Taliban had angered the people through a combination of repression and lousy government services. I interview Afghans who criticize U.S. destruction of civilian infrastructure and the thousands of civilian deaths. But they had lived through a civil war of horrendous cruelty, and by comparison, the United States doesn't seem so bad. However, the Afghans expect the United States to expel the Taliban and then leave. But that was never the U.S. intention.

Even back then it was obvious that Afghanistan would become a long-term occupation. Global Exchange executive director Medea Benjamin told me in 2002, "I think we're getting ourselves deeper and deeper into a very negative relationship with the Muslim world. One of the reasons many Muslims resent the United States is its presence in the territory that is not its own. This will only fuel the resentment."[13]

The United States isn't the first world power to have illusions about conquering Afghanistan. In the days before World War I, Afghanistan was a chess piece in the "great game" played by imperialist powers. British, French, German, Russian, and Ottoman empires competed to control natural resources, sea lanes, and military bases throughout the region. Things haven't changed much. Afghanistan borders key oil-producing countries, Iran and Turkmenistan. As the proposed UNOCAL gas pipeline showed, he who controls Afghanistan also controls a vital route for Caspian Sea oil. I don't think Bush invaded Afghanistan in order to build a pipeline. But once the 9/11 attack occurred, he was happy to expand the empire's sphere of influence. As a direct result of the Afghan war, the United States established new bases or landing rights in six neighboring countries.

Having driven the Taliban from power, the United States had to install a pro-American regime in Kabul. Hamid Karzai, the scion of a powerful Pashtun family, filled the bill. The U.S. government cemented cooperation between Karzai and the Northern Alliance, the mujahedeen remnants still fighting the Taliban. The Northern Alliance financed their rebellion with heroin profits and maintained a fundamentalist ideology.[14] They had no more commitment to democracy than the Taliban. But, for the moment, they were pro-American, and that's all that mattered.

The people of Afghanistan became quickly disillusioned with the lawless greed of the pro-U.S. liberators. In January 2002, I interviewed Obeidullah Shanawaz, a wealthy farmer who complained that a Northern Alliance commander had stolen his four-wheel-drive car. He says the commander and 17 soldiers came to his house, claiming the car belonged to the Taliban. "When I showed him my ownership papers, they put me in handcuffs and threatened to arrest me." No one in Kabul could get the car returned.[15] More than one prisoner landed in the infamous, U.S-run Bagram prison because of similar accusations.

During my 2009 trip to Afghanistan, an Afghan-American NGO worker told me she had just experienced a similar incident. One night she and her driver went into an area of Kabul where many displaced people live. She found the headman of the community and gave him local currency worth $300 to buy food and medical supplies. He carefully counted it out with other displaced villagers observing. The local police commander soon got word, stopped her car, and demanded a similar payment. When she refused, he accused her of being a prostitute and funding the Taliban—the two worst crimes he could think of. Armed police surrounded her car.

Luckily, the woman knew a cousin of President Karzai. After a few tense minutes, a higher-ranking police commander showed up. The local repeated his charge that he had caught her providing money to the Taliban, and that she was a prostitute on her way to assignations with refugees. The story didn't make any sense on its face. (Poor refugees and the Taliban collaborate to hire American prostitutes?) The higher commander ordered her released, and she got back safely to the hotel. The incident illustrates how Afghan authorities routinely operate. Had the woman not been highly connected, or if she wasn't a Westerner, the outcome could have been quite different. Not a few of the tips received by U.S. forces about Taliban activity come from corrupt officials seeking revenge against rivals. Many Afghans hate the Taliban, but the insurgents seem like honest freedom fighters compared to many Karzai government officials.

WITHIN A FEW MONTHS of their arrival in 2001, U.S. troops were fighting a tough counterinsurgency war in Afghanistan. Former U.S. Marine Rick Reyes, who was stationed near the city of Kandahar during the opening months of the campaign, tells me most Afghans own an AK-47. "There's no way to know if these guys are combatants or not. So you kind of make yourself a target and wait around until you get shot at. At that point, there's still that question: maybe they're just pissed off because we're here."[16]

The United States uses air superiority to wreck horrendous damage on enemy forces—when they can be found. Afghans can recount numerous examples of air attacks that killed civilians mistaken for Taliban. Each incident has a similar pattern. The U.S. military announces a successful attack on a Taliban position and the death of militants. Afghan government officials angrily criticize the raid as having killed civilians. The U.S. military denies the claim, but promises to investigate. Weeks or even months later, hoping the outcry has calmed down, the United States admits some of the dead were indeed civilians, unfortunate casualties of war.

The cover-up sometimes works with the American public, but it's been a disaster for Afghan civilians. For example, on August 22, 2008, U.S. planes supposedly bombed a Taliban stronghold. Later investigations by the United Nations and the Afghan government showed 90 civilians killed, including 60 sleeping children. The military initially claimed 25 militants were killed, but eventually admitted civilians died as well. It never admitted the accuracy of the UN count.[17]

In 2009 the U.S. military modified its rules of engagement to lessen reliance on air strikes and reduce the number of civilian casualties. Without close air support, however, the U. S. military loses one of its main technological advantages. Troops on the ground complained bitterly. Thus the United States faced one of the main contradictions of being an occupying power: if it tries to wage a humanitarian war and not kill civilians, it faces military setbacks. If it uses overwhelming firepower to win, it loses politically.

Many Afghans say indiscriminate killing of civilians constitutes terrorism. But U.S. and Western military officials angrily deny the charge, because they don't *intentionally* kill civilians. But as Human

Rights Watch notes, "NATO operations . . . appear to have violated the laws of war. While there is no evidence suggesting that coalition or NATO forces have intentionally directed attacks against civilians, in a number of cases international forces have conducted indiscriminate attacks or otherwise failed to take adequate precautions to prevent harm to civilians."[18]

The Taliban and other insurgents also use terrorist tactics. They train suicide bombers and plant roadside bombs intending to kill foreign troops but know that civilians will also die. In other cases, they detonate suicide bombs in markets or on street corners to prove that the United States can't protect ordinary people. The insurgents continue to use tactics they learned as U.S.-supported mujahedeen. Human Rights Watch writes, "Many civilians have been specifically targeted by the insurgents, including aid workers, doctors, day laborers, mechanics, students, clerics, and civilian government employees such as teachers and engineers."

The insurgents include not only the Taliban led by Mullah Omar but also forces loyal to Gulbuddin Hekmatyar and Jalaluddin Haqqani, another mujahedeen veteran. In January 2010, insurgents showed a new level of sophistication when a Jordanian double agent, supposedly working for the CIA, blew up seven CIA officers on a base in Afghanistan. Reuel Marc Gerecht, a former CIA officer, writes that the insurgents "did to us exactly what we intended to do to them: use a mole for a lethal strike against high-value targets."[19]

A few days after the incident, the Pakistani Taliban claimed credit for the bombing. It released a video shot before the attack showing the double agent sitting with Pakistani Taliban chief Hakimullah Mehsud. The Pakistani Taliban didn't even exist until a few years ago. It, along with other right-wing fundamentalist groups, gained strength from the popular anger against the U.S. occupation of Afghanistan and its meddling in Pakistan. When I reported from Islamabad in October 1999, such parties regularly lost parliamentary elections and had few followers. Today they constitute a major threat to the government of Pakistan and the entire region. They have won local Pakistani elections and have mounted a serious armed insurgency against the government. In the name of combating terrorism, the United States has managed to spread the problem even further.

THE U.S. WAR IN AFGHANISTAN has fostered massive and systemic corruption by both Afghans and Americans. A UN Office on Drugs and Crime report estimated that Afghans paid $2.5 billion in bribes in 2009, almost 25 percent of the country's entire gross domestic product. About one quarter of Afghans surveyed said they had to pay bribes to obtain government services, most often to police, judges, and politicians. But they also saw foreign NGOs and international organizations as corrupt.[20] Nor are Afghan officials alone.

Both the U.S. military and civilian contracting process is fraught with waste and fraud. Since 2001, the U.S. government has allocated $38 billion in aid to Afghanistan; 53 percent of that went for civilian projects.[21] Afghanistan's foreign minister, Rangin Dadfar Spanta, sharply criticized how U.S. aid is spent in his country. He told me in an exclusive interview that only "$10 or $20" of every $100 reaches its intended recipients.[22]

I investigated one specific program that is typical of U.S. civilian contracts. The agricultural storage facility in Nangarhar Province, built in 2004, was supposed to win the hearts and minds of the Afghan people. The U.S. government paid for its construction along with several other so-called market centers that would enable farmers to store crops and boost exports to nearby Pakistan. But construction and design flaws left it unusable, one of many dozens of similar failures around the country. In 2003, the U.S. government planned to build 145 such market centers to help increase farm exports. A major Washington DC company, Chemonics International, won the bid for the $145 million program—known as Rebuilding Agricultural Markets Program, or RAMP—that ran for three years. Chemonics then subcontracted the training and construction work to other Americans, who in turn subcontracted to numerous Afghan companies, who did the actual work. At each level, the subcontractors deducted costs for salaries, office expenses, and security.

Only a small percentage of the original RAMP contract money actually reached farmers and other intended recipients, according to Afzal Rashid, a former senior advisor for the ministry of finance, who now lives in Sacramento, California.[23] The exact percentage may never be known because neither Chemonics nor the U.S. government tracks such figures. Moreover, many of the market centers have deteriorated or are not being used for their original purpose. Chemonics spokeswoman Lisa Gihring wrote me in an email, "More recent anecdotal information indicates that a vast majority of these centers have contributed to their original goals and, thus, thousands of Afghan farmers have benefited from their development."[24] That's not exactly a ringing defense of the program, which many Afghan farmers consider a miserable failure.

Oxfam, the respected British nonprofit aid group, reports that the U.S. Agency for International Development (USAID) awards more than half of its Afghan aid to just five U.S. private contractors with close political ties in Washington.[25] They include KBR, the Louis Berger Group, Bearing Point, DynCorp International, and Chemonics International. USAID allows contractors to budget $500,000 annual salaries and benefits for high-ranking employees, and $200,000 for lower-ranking administrators. Hardship and hazard pay boost all expatriate employee salaries by as much as 70 percent. By comparison, the average Afghan civil servant receives less than $1,000 a month. Rashid and other critics say waste and fraud are built into the system. Expatriate employees bank most of their salary because companies pay for employee travel and living expenses. "In a lot of cases the money goes from one bank account in the U.S. to another account in the U.S.," and never helps the economy of Afghanistan, says Rashid.

USAID has a truly mind-boggling defense: it doesn't really matter how much of the original money reaches the intended recipients so long as some gets spent in Afghanistan. Jerry Kryschtal, a contracting officer in Afghanistan for USAID, tells me it's acceptable "if about 50 percent of the original contract money reaches Afghanistan." After all, he reasons, that money pays guards, cooks, drivers, and other local staff—and thus helps the country's economy.[26] By that logic, an American city should be happy if a contractor constructs a new courthouse that collapses so long as he spends half the contract money in local hotels and restaurants.

AFTER THE 2001 U.S. INVASION, Mullah Nizami fled to Peshawar with his family. He continued to be a spokesman for the illusive Mullah Omar, who had also escaped Afghanistan, reportedly driving off on a motorcycle minutes ahead of U.S. troops. But in June 2007 Nizami changed sides, much to the chagrin of his Taliban comrades, who tried to minimize the impact of his defection. A Taliban spokesperson claimed Nizami "is mentally sick. He had some cultural relations to the Taliban, but he was not an important person."[27]

Nizami tells me that he received a personal message from President Karzai offering amnesty if he returned to Kabul. According to Nizami, the president specifically praised him for saving the TV archives. Nizami has attempted to broker several deals between the government and insurgents. But he's critical of the process. "Verbally the peace process is going on, but practically we are seeing different things." He complains that for him and fellow defectors, there is no program to provide jobs, housing, or even meals, as promised by the government. He's also pessimistic because the insurgents seem to be gaining strength as indicated by stepped up military attacks. "Today they are more powerful than before and everybody knows that." He echoes the position of Karzai and the United States: the United States must remain in Afghanistan to train the army and police.

And I was about to meet an antiwar advocate who feels the same way.

SANTWANA DASGUPTA is a force of nature. Born in India, she moved to Minneapolis at age 19. She had a successful career in corporate America, working for American Express, and then started a new life working for NGOs. When we meet, she is volunteer executive director of Afghans4Tomorrow, which runs a girls' school and other educational projects. We talk in Kabul late into the night over warmed curry, Coca-Cola, and rum. Dasgupta considers herself an antiwar progressive. That's why her anger at the antiwar movement surprises me. "These groups like Code Pink call for immediate withdrawal of American troops from Afghanistan," she says. "But what about American responsibility to develop Afghanistan?"[28]

She argues that immediate withdrawal of troops would lead to a collapse of the Afghan government and triumph of the Taliban, setting back whatever progress had been made by Afghans over the past nine years. She argues that the peace movement should demand a genuine development strategy. The United States should focus on improving the lives of civilians, while keeping enough troops to train the Afghan military and police. Then the United States should negotiate a date for eventual withdrawal. I fully understand her views. If the U.S. military pulls out quickly, projects such as hers will end. The Taliban would never tolerate foreigners teaching girls, or even the existence of girls' schools.

We agree that the Afghan people must determine their own future, but sharply disagree on how. I tell her that the United States did not occupy Afghanistan to protect women's rights or help develop the country. The United States will never develop Afghanistan's economy except as part of a militarily strategy. After all, it once had an opportunity to do so. After the U.S.-backed mujahedeen defeated the Red Army in 1989, the United States didn't pour aid money and civilian personnel into Afghanistan. By the mid 1990s, the United States abandoned the country to the battling warlords and the Taliban. The United States has no recent history of developing an impoverished third world country it has conquered.[29] Once the United States "wins," it abandons the winner to the vicissitudes of the free market.

We went back and forth in the discussion. Neither of us changed our core position. But Dasgupta does make an important point. The people of Afghanistan do need assistance, although not the kind they're getting from major U.S. aid contractors. They need schools, hospitals, and other infrastructure destroyed by the civil war, the Taliban, and the United States. The peace movement also tends to forget civilians once the United States withdraws troops. I would like to see a political settlement that allows for independent economic development and the promotion of human rights. The question is how do we get there?

First of all, we have to understand the political realities. The current regime in Kabul is no protector of the rights of women or anyone else. President Karzai has little power outside Kabul. He relies on warlords for political support. Their views on the economy, women, and human rights differ little from those of the insurgents. Women enjoy relatively more rights in Kabul, but those rights disappear in other cities under nominal government control. Female students at the University of Kabul told me women can't attend graduate school even in the capital, and there are no jobs for them once they obtain undergraduate degrees. Afghans are growing increasingly unhappy with a prolonged U.S. presence. Starting in 2009 a majority of Americans opposed the war, and this seems unlikely to change. No matter what, the United States will eventually have to wind down its military presence, and Afghans will have to negotiate their own political settlement. The question is how many Afghans and Americans will die before that happens?

The basis for a negotiated peace plan exists. Taliban leaders have said on several occasions that they have severed ties with Osama bin Laden and al Qaeda.[30] They have also offered to give legally binding guarantees not to interfere in other countries' affairs in return for the withdrawal of foreign troops. In 2009 Mullah Omar said a Taliban-controlled Afghanistan wouldn't be a base for international terrorism. He said, "We assure all countries that the Islamic Emirate of Afghanistan, as a responsible force, will not extend its hand to cause jeopardy to others."[31]

But what if the insurgents are lying, and they do still have ties with al Qaeda? Consider the objective situation that will confront them. After a U.S. withdrawal *any* new government will have to focus on resolving the country's huge security and economic problems—and will be in no position to plot terrorist attacks on the United States. For its part, al Qaeda doesn't need Afghanistan as a base of operations anymore. The group no longer has strong central leadership, having devolved into a series of local cells operating in far-flung parts of the world, from Yemen to east Africa to Pakistan. Afghanistan simply won't play the same role as in the 1990s.

In December 2009, the Obama administration announced plans to send 30,000 more troops to Afghanistan, bringing the total to 100,000 in 2010. The cost of the U.S. war will surge to $100 billion per year. Obama pledged to begin reducing U.S. troop levels by July 2011 but left lots of room to change course if the war goes badly. At no time did the administration agree to a total withdrawal of troops and mercenaries, and a closing of all U.S. bases. The Obama administration faced sharp criticism of the escalation even from within its own ranks. U.S. ambassador to Afghanistan Karl Eikenberry wrote internal cables saying that Afghan police and army won't be ready to handle security even after a few years. He wrote that the Karzai government expects the United States to stay permanently. "They assume we covet their territory for a never-ending 'war on terror' and for military bases to use against surrounding powers."[32] Hmmmm. Wonder how the Afghans came up with *that* idea?

The United States can use the Iraqi Status of Forces Agreement as a rough model to quickly withdraw its forces.[33] The United States would agree to rapidly withdraw all troops and mercenaries and close all bases by certain legally binding dates. The U.S. and Western powers would guarantee economic aid to be administered by the United Nations and independent NGOs. Those civilian agencies would be guaranteed funding and security in cooperation with the new Afghan government so long as they remain unattached to a military effort. Such guarantees would spur the various insurgent factions to sit down for talks.

I don't have illusions that the negotiated settlement will produce a democratic government that respects human rights. But at least there is a chance for peace and stability. Over time, the Afghan people themselves will develop their own political and economic system, not one imposed by imperial powers. And the potential for such a settlement exists. In March 2010 representatives of insurgent Gulbuddin Hekmatyar met with President Karzai in Kabul to discuss a peace plan. Press reports indicate both sides had substantial agreement but couldn't agree on the issue of withdrawal of foreign troops.[34]

To date, both the Bush and Obama administrations have not offered any meaningful concessions. The United States attempts to win over moderate insurgents by offering them money and possible posts in the government. But Mullah Nizami says, "Paying the low-level [Taliban] may work temporarily, but it won't solve the main problems. There is so much corruption and no laws. In many areas the Taliban have been able to bring security and justice, which the government has not done. Even if some fighters turn, they will turn back again when they understand that their lives are not better."[35] He says the war won't end until Karzai and the United States are willing to change.

Mullah Nizami gets up to leave the room where we are talking. He once again wipes his lips with his beard. As he shakes my hand, he offers one last appeal to America. "We want a peaceful Afghanistan," he tells me, "and it won't come through U.S. bombing."

eight

Media Distortions, Obama's Policies, and Ending the War on Terrorism

TALIBAN PUSH POPPY PRODUCTION TO A RECORD AGAIN
—*New York Times* headline, Aug. 26, 2007

HUNDREDS OF ARTICLES containing similar messages have appeared in major U.S. media. By now, we all know that opium production and heroin smuggling are controlled by the Taliban pursuing its terrorist war against the United States. It's all true except for one small part. Insurgents don't control the drug trade, U.S. allies do. The intentional government manipulation and media misreporting of this story tells us a lot about what's wrong with the Global War on Terrorism.

I've been covering the heroin story in Afghanistan since January 2002, just three months after the U.S. invasion. Since the beginning of the U.S. occupation, the drug trade was controlled by criminals working with warlords loyal to the United States. The CIA has kept known drug kingpins on its payroll because they helped maintain U.S. rule. It just took a long time for the U.S. media to report it, and even now, we don't get the full story.[1]

IN 2009 I visited the heavily fortified UN Office of Drugs and Crime (UNODC) compound in Kabul. Workers were putting the finishing touches on a new blast wall inside the existing eight-foot-high blast wall. One couldn't be too careful in Kabul. Jean Luc Lemahieu, head of the Afghanistan office, came out to greet me with a wide smile and firm handshake. We sat down in his office and he provided some numbers. According to 2009 UNODC figures, the insurgents directly control only about $125 million of the country's $4.4 billion retail heroin trade. That's 2.8 percent of the total. The CIA and Defense Intelligence Agency put the Taliban control at $75 million, or 1.7 percent.[2] At least 97 percent of the drug trade in Afghanistan is controlled by someone other than insurgents. "There are people in this government who are the big architects," Lemahieu told me. "That's what's dangerous."[3]

Who are some of the main traffickers? Former defense minister Marshal Muhammad Qasim Fahim, who became first vice president after the 2009 elections, once shipped his heroin to Russia in a government cargo plane, which then returned stuffed with cash.[4] Ahmad Wali Karzai, half-brother of the president, amassed a fortune by controlling key transportation routes for shipping heroin through Kandahar Province while on the CIA payroll. The U.S. government tolerated his drug smuggling because of his support for a CIA-commanded militia, the Kandahar Strike Force. The strike force not only attacked insurgents but also murdered the provincial police chief in Kandahar in a dispute over the arrest of the brother of a strike force member.[5] Ahmad Wali Karzai called the allegations of drug running "baseless."[6]

In Kabul I interviewed Mohammad Zafar, Afghanistan's deputy antinarcotics minister. He also denied that Karzai or any other high level official is involved in drug dealing. "If any person is involved, even the brother of the president, he will be captured by the government," he told me. "We don't have any evidence in this regard."

An anonymous former CIA official is more straightforward. "Virtually every significant Afghan figure has had brushes with the drug trade," he said. "If you are looking for Mother Teresa, she doesn't live in Afghanistan."[7]

Afzal Rashid, a former senior advisor to the Afghan ministry of finance whom we met in the last chapter, told me the pro-U.S. warlords use drug money to finance their militias, grease their patronage machines, and bribe government officials. "The whole Ministry of Interior was corrupt in its relations with the drug dealers," he said. The U.S. government and President Karzai ignore the high-level drug traffickers because their support is needed for the U.S. war effort. "I'm sure the U.S. Army looked the other way," he said. "Maybe the warlords were helping identify al Qaeda."

The Taliban *do* profit from the drug trade by taxing poppy farmers and extorting protection money from smugglers passing through their territory. But they don't control the national smuggling rings, where the real money is made. Criminal gangs and pro-U.S. warlords control that part of the business and happily collude with the insurgents on buying, selling, and shipping heroin. "The parliament issues statements that the international community wants to hear," says UNODC official Lemahieu. "And then at night they are negotiating trade agreements with people who are considered their enemy."

If I can walk into the UNODC and other offices in Kabul to get this information, why was nothing appearing in the *New York Times, Wall Street Journal*, or on CNN for so many years?[8] Bits and pieces came out, and critical reporting improved as the U.S. officials sought to discredit President Karzai after 2007. But even today, U.S. reporters haven't pulled the entire story together because it undercuts the very rationale for the occupation of Afghanistan and the wider War on Terrorism, as I found out on a journey to Jalalabad.

ON A CLEAR SUMMER DAY in 2009, I drive out of Kabul to interview opium farmers. "The road from Kabul to Jalalabad is perfectly safe today," my colleague and fixer Najibullah tells me. "It hasn't been bombed for four days." Driving in a beat-up old Toyota, Najibullah, the driver, and I are all wearing traditional white baggy pants and long-tailed shirts so we can slip through government checkpoints and confuse any lurking insurgents. I apparently look Afghan enough that we are waived through every military and police checkpoint. Our destination is a farm outside Jalalabad, near the Pakistan border.

Driving out of Kabul we quickly approach a deep valley with high, craggy mountains on either side. Water and wind have carved the mountains into steep, jagged cliffs. River water has eaten away parts of the mountain walls, creating precariously balanced shelves of rock that seem ready to break off at any moment. The mountain pass reminds me why conquering Afghanistan has never been easy. A few people atop the cliffs armed with nothing more than rocks to start an avalanche could hold off a conquering ground army for weeks. Conquering the opium/heroin trade in Afghanistan has proven to be just as difficult.

Jalalabad has long been an agricultural center for eastern Afghanistan. Green, verdant fields irrigated by local rivers pop up in the distance. The U.S. government and some Afghan officials are trying to get local farmers to stop growing opium poppy in favor of apricots and other fruit. We drive out of the city on rutted dirt roads to a farmhouse. There I meet Ebadullah Ebad. The craggy-faced farmer wraps a traditional scarf around his head to protect against the burning sun. Ebad and his family had grown opium poppies on their small farm in the 1990s, stopped in 2000–2001 when the Taliban banned

it, and then resumed harvesting from 2001–6. They've stopped growing poppy for now, having planted vegetables and an apricot orchard.
Understanding the reasons for their stopping and starting is crucial to
understanding the U.S. misinformation campaign about the heroin
trade.

Throughout the 1980s, mujahedeen fighting the Soviet occupation of Afghanistan partially financed their war by selling heroin.
When the Taliban seized power in 1996, it also took a cut of the
illegal trafficking. But under tremendous international pressure, the
Taliban agreed to stop poppy cultivation in June 2000. The Taliban
told farmers that growing poppy was un-Islamic. For the first and
only time in recent Afghan history, poppy cultivation stopped almost
completely. However, the Northern Alliance fighting the Taliban
continued the drug trade. "The Northern Alliance has always been
producing drugs," former Pakistani general Shaukat Qadir tells me in
Rawalpindi, Pakistan. "It was never a moral issue. It was economics."[9]

In October 2001 the United States needed the Northern Alliance
warlords to put an Afghan face on the U.S. occupation. As the U.S.
military and the Northern Alliance warlords marched into Kabul,
the narco networks immediately expanded. By the next growing
season, poppy was back in bloom, and Afghanistan quickly became
the world's number one heroin supplier. It was simple free market
economics. The West had a demand for heroin. Afghanistan had
hardworking farmers and entrepreneurial drug traffickers who could
match supply with demand. Once the United States invaded, there
were no more of those pesky government regulations to bother the
narco-capitalists.

The misinformation campaign began immediately. How could
the sudden resurgence of the heroin trade be explained? According to U.S. and other Western governments, the Taliban had never
really stopped heroin trafficking. They had stopped opium growing, you see, but had been stockpiling heroin in warehouses and

then flooded the market after the U.S. invasion. The major media swallowed the story without doing much firsthand investigation. For example, *Wall Street Journal* reporters based in Europe wrote an article claiming that the heroin stockpiles "are controlled by the Taliban, al Qaeda, and allied drug barons."[10] When I checked out the story, however, officials in Afghanistan and Pakistan told me that criminal elements were dumping massive quantities of heroin, fearing the uncertainty of a new regime. U.S. military and government sources never provided proof that the Taliban warehoused massive amounts of heroin.

And so the narrative was born. Yes, heroin production is a growing problem because it became "a major source of financing for the Taliban," as claimed by the *New York Times* and virtually every other major media outlet.[11] A few reporters didn't follow the accepted story, such as *New York Times* Afghanistan correspondent Carlotta Gall. As far back as 2004, she named a number of Karzai cabinet ministers and governors "widely rumored to profit from the [drug] trade."[12] Similar stories occasionally appeared in the *Times* or other major media. At their best, the articles mentioned that both Karzai officials and the Taliban benefited from the drug trade. But when no one in Washington became angry at the revelations and Karzai's warlords remained closely allied with the U.S. military, the stories had no impact on policy or on the dominant narrative.

Suspicious activity at the highest levels unfolded almost immediately after the U.S. invasion. For example, Abdul Rahman, Afghanistan's minister of aviation and tourism, was murdered at the Kabul airport on February 14, 2002. Karzai initially blamed the murder on six top government and intelligence officials associated with the Northern Alliance. Reports at the time indicated the murder resulted from a dispute over lucrative drug smuggling routes. The case against the officials was eventually dropped, however, with the claim that the minister was killed by angry pilgrims waiting for their plane to Mecca.[13] The U.S. media accepted that account, and the issue was dropped.

THOSE EARLY YEARS of the U.S. occupation were boom times for the Ebad family farmers. In 2004 they were growing opium poppy, which was fetching $220 a kilo, a fortune for small farmers. "It made economic sense," Ebad told me. "With that money, we solved all of our problems." Local drug traffickers loaned him money to plant the crop. "Three times, I got money in advance because I needed it. When my opium was ready for harvest, I gave it to them in return for the advance money."

Ebad explained that the traffickers shipped the opium to primitive labs, where it was turned into heroin for eventual shipment to nearby Pakistan. Each step of the process was protected by local police and political officials. They, in turn, were protected by networks of traffickers reaching all the way to the Karzai cabinet. For farmer Ebad, abandoning poppy cultivation was a straight-up economic decision. Squatting in his field where the poppies used to grow, he told me when the price of raw opium dropped, he welcomed U.S. efforts to help his family grow other crops. And, he said with a chuckle, if his new crops aren't profitable enough, "I'll return to planting poppy."

MAINSTREAM MEDIA COVERAGE of the heroin issue began shifting in the later part of the Bush administration's second term. President Karzai, hoping to stay in power after an eventual U.S. withdrawal, began espousing some nationalist and populist views. He condemned U.S. air attacks that killed civilians and refused to allow aerial spraying of deadly pesticides to destroy poppy fields. In response to what

Washington considered anti-American positions, U.S. officials began leaking unfavorable reports about the Karzai government's drug ties. Relying mostly on CIA, State Department, and similar sources, a 2007 front page *New York Times* article revealed that some U.S. allies in Afghanistan were drug lords. But the *Times* put the onus on both the insurgents and Karzai. "Major dealers, often with ties both to government officials and the Taliban, operate virtually at will." The article also contained what was becoming the standard excuse for U.S. cooperation with drug lords. "American officials say that the postwar chaos left them with no choice but to work with militia leaders involved in drug dealing."[14]

After Obama's election in 2008, negative stories about Karzai appeared more frequently. Now we have two types of evil Afghans. The Taliban are still responsible for most of the heroin trade, but corrupt Karzai officials contribute to the problem. The major media have yet to thoroughly investigate the U.S. government role in all of this.

WHY ARE THE STORIES SO SIMILAR from media supposedly in fierce competition with one another? If all the media run variations of the same story, isn't there a conspiracy at the highest levels? I wish it were that simple.

The fact is, U.S. rulers impact media coverage in a number of pernicious ways without having to resort to secret meetings in parking garages. The first line of defense is ideological. Mainstream foreign correspondents receive top salaries and garner lots of prestige. As I described in *Target Iraq: What the News Media Didn't Tell You*, anyone who writes too critically of U.S. foreign policy doesn't stay employed. You don't win a Pulitzer Prize for questioning the basic assumptions of empire. You do advance your career, however, by cultivating high-level diplomatic, military, and intelligence sources.[15]

In the aftermath of 9/11, the Bush administration pushed all the right media buttons. It appealed to patriotism and reporters' fears that they might be out of sync with public opinion.

The mainstream media followed the administration's line that the United States was under assault by a vicious enemy at home and abroad. When the CIA and other agencies leaked classified documents showing that Saddam Hussein had weapons of mass destruction and ties to al Qaeda, almost all the mainstream media ran the stories without deeper investigation.

When reporters occasionally run major stories highly unpopular in Washington, they feel the full wrath of the empire. When CBS TV aired a story questioning President George W. Bush's service in the National Guard during the Vietnam War, even someone with the prestige of Dan Rather came under attack. Eventually Rather was hounded into leaving CBS.[16] As the major media consolidate into fewer and fewer oligopolies, companies cut back newsroom staff and eliminate bureaus. Foreign correspondents, including those who might consider themselves politically liberal, fear causing too much controversy. They keep their heads down and their hands outstretched for a paycheck.

Editors also use sharply different criteria for evaluating the validity of information critical of U.S. power. No reporter gets fired for accurately reporting statements from high American officials, even if they are outright lies. But you may lose your job if you write a story too critical of those same high officials, unless the source is some other high-level official. I've written articles about the Afghan drug trade only to have editors cut the sections naming Karzai ministers and their links to the U.S. government. That information would be included in the story, I was told, only if confirmed by the DEA, CIA, or a similar Washington source. That, of course, gives the government virtual censorship power over controversial stories.

The dominant narrative on any given story trickles down to local media as well. After my 2002 trip to Afghanistan and publication in a local magazine of an article about the U.S.-allied warlords' involvement in the drug trade, I was contacted by a local TV reporter. She did a long interview and aired a story about the growing danger of the heroin trade. She systematically edited out every comment I made about pro-U.S. warlords, however, and inserted her own opinion that the Taliban was at fault. And she had a lot of editing to do, because I mentioned it in almost every other sentence.

THE AFGHAN DRUG TRADE STORY is just one example of how the government and media manipulate public opinion. Perhaps the most egregious example is how they distort the term "terrorist." As used in the United States today, the word has become almost meaningless.

On February 18, 2010, Andrew Joseph Stack flew a small plane into an office building housing the Internal Revenue Service (IRS) in Austin, Texas. Earlier that day, Stack wrote a diatribe on his Web page against the IRS and the federal government. "Violence not only is the answer," he wrote, "it is the only answer." He ended his blog post by writing "Joe Stack (1956–2010)."[17] Stack clearly engaged in a political suicide mission, resulting in the murder of one IRS employee and injuries to 13 people in the building. Yet local officials and mainstream media refused to call this an act of terrorism. "I consider this a criminal act by a lone individual," said Austin police chief Art Acevedo.[18] Had Stack survived, police would have read him his Miranda rights and charged him with murder.

Compare that with a similar incident involving a Palestinian American. On November 5, 2009, Maj. Nidal Malik Hasan, an Army psychiatrist, opened fire on fellow soldiers in Fort Hood, Texas, killing 13 and wounding 29. He strongly opposed U.S. military action in Afghanistan and Iraq. Conservatives immediately opened a campaign to label this a terrorist incident. Senator Joe Lieberman told

Fox News, "There are very, very strong warning signs here that Dr. Hasan had become an Islamist extremist and therefore that this was a terrorist act."[19] In Lieberman's worldview, extremism comes only from the Muslim world, not right-wing white people with persecution complexes and pilots' licenses.

Either everyone using violence against civilians for political ends is a terrorist, or none are. Given the massive amount of confusion and misinformation on the topic, I would prefer that the term "terrorism" be dropped altogether. But as a working journalist, I know that won't likely be adopted by the mainstream media anytime soon.

I had an interesting radio debate with a *Wall Street Journal* reporter on precisely this topic. He argued that right-wing, domestic terrorists present little threat to national security, while Muslim terrorists are clearly part of a much more serious, worldwide effort. So Muslim terrorism must be pursued much more vigorously, he argued. That view, however, requires us to set aside the Constitution in order to racially profile Arabs and ignore their rights to due process of law. But the political logic of the argument is flawed as well. There is no worldwide conspiracy by Muslims to overthrow the U.S. government. There are isolated cells and individuals with little popular support and no ability to achieve their ideological goals. Treating them as enemy combatants without legal rights elevates the status of criminals acting under the cover of religion.

But the conversation with the *Journal* reporter raised an important question. What should the government do when faced with individuals actually engaging in terrorist actions?

AHMED RESSAM had been planning the operation for months. The Algerian born, unemployed laborer, and small-time thief had become increasingly radicalized living in France and later in Canada. He traveled to an al Qaeda training camp in Afghanistan, learned the basics of bomb making, and selected his target. He planned to leave a suitcase bomb in a public terminal at Los Angeles Airport with the potential to kill and maim dozens of civilians.

The fog rolled into the harbor as a nervous Ressam boarded the ferry to cross from British Columbia to Washington State. He carried bomb components in the wheel well of his rental car. But on the Washington side, a suspicious border patrol officer asked for his ID. As agents searched the car, Ressam ran, but he was captured quickly. Authorities found explosives, timers, and fuses in the car trunk. It was December 14, 1999.[20]

Ahmed Ressam was arrested, read his Miranda rights, and eventually gave a full confession. He had enlisted support of a small group of like-minded extremists in Canada. On April 6, 2001, sixteen months after his arrest, Ressam was convicted in a Los Angeles federal court on nine counts, including conspiracy to commit terrorism. He was later sentenced to 22 years because he initially offered to testify against other conspirators, but an appeals court ordered the sentence extended when he stopped cooperating.

Ressam had no popular support among American Muslims, and his actions were immediately condemned by Muslim groups. The Council on American-Islamic Relations (CAIR) wrote in a press release immediately after the arrest, "Any Muslim who plans, attempts or carries out a terrorist attack would be acting outside the boundaries of his or her faith, and would be repudiated and condemned by our community. American Muslims would urge that any such individuals be prosecuted to the full extent of the law."[21] Unlike some terrorist suspects who were tortured or otherwise brutalized, Ressam never became a cause célèbre because his treatment was perceived as fair.

When the U.S. government had convincing evidence of a terrorist plot, the police and judicial systems worked. Federal Judge John

Coughenour, who presided over the trial, noted that in Ressam's case "there were no secret proceedings, no indefinite detention, no denial of counsel . . . The tragedy of Sept. 11 shook our sense of security and made us realize that we, too, are vulnerable to acts of terrorism. Unfortunately, some believe that this threat renders our Constitution obsolete . . . If that view is allowed to prevail, the terrorists will have won."[22]

Prior to September 11, 2001, the U.S. government dealt with domestic terrorism as a criminal issue. Contrary to myth, the civilian judicial system is perfectly capable of punishing terrorists. If anything, the system is stacked against criminal defendants advocating unpopular views about Muslims and the Middle East.

In 1987 the federal government arrested eight pro-Palestinian immigrant activists in Los Angeles. The government attempted to deport them, not for committing crimes, but for raising money and passing out the newspaper of the Popular Front for the Liberation of Palestine (PFLP), one of the groups within the PLO. The PFLP was not then listed on the State Department list of terrorist organizations. Even William Webster, the FBI director at the time, testified before Congress that the government had no proof of terrorist activity. He admitted, "If these individuals had been United States citizens, there would not have been a basis for their arrest."[23] The LA Eight, as they became known, fought for the next 20 years to stay in the United States, and for their first amendment right to peacefully speak and organize. After numerous legal rulings against the government case and political outrage in the Palestinian community, the feds finally dropped deportation charges in 2007.

But such trumped-up cases aren't part of the dialogue in Washington DC. Politicians prefer to stoke post-9/11 panic by claiming virtually every imam and mosque is a potential terrorist threat. The Bush administration adopted a series of unprecedented measures that asserted the government's right to detain anyone without trial and torture them—all in the name of wartime necessity. Such policies alienate significant numbers of Arabs and Muslims who oppose terrorism. The actions turn terrorists into heroes and help recruit new people to the extremist cause.

President Obama was supposed to change all that.

THE 2008 PRESIDENTIAL ELECTION offered the chance to get rid of the phony Global War on Terrorism. Tens of millions of Americans voted against Bush and the Republican policies of the previous eight years. Candidate Barak Obama captured the popular imagination by promising to end the Iraq war and restore the rule of law. On his first day in office Obama signed an executive order to close the Guantanamo prison within a year. Obama promised to withdraw combat troops from Iraq in 2010 and pull all troops out by December 31, 2011, as specified in the Status of Forces agreement agreed to by President Bush.

The administration quietly dropped the use of the term "Global War on Terrorism." Yet Obama continued to support the basic assumptions of GWOT. Citing the fight against terrorism, in the spring of 2009, Obama sent 12,000 more troops to Afghanistan and then an additional 30,000 in 2010. The administration widened the covert war in Pakistan. It continued to accuse Iran of planning to build a nuclear bomb and kept the "military option" on the table for possible future attacks.[24]

In domestic policy, the Obama administration announced it would return to the rule of law and try accused terrorists arrested in the United States in civilian courts. However, it faced tremendous pressure from right-wing politicians, intelligence agencies, and the military. Republican leaders criticized the administration for reading

Miranda rights to alleged terrorists arrested inside the United States, although that had been U.S. policy for years. Former vice-presidential candidate Sarah Palin famously said, "We need a commander-in-chief, not a professor of law."[25]

Victoria Toensing, a deputy assistant attorney general in the Reagan administration, invoked wartime necessity to argue that terrorists have no right to a civilian trial. "Since 9/11 we know that terrorists want to destroy our democratic government and murder us . . . Constitutionally evolving protections . . . have created a rich array of legal maneuvers that terrorists can use and abuse, not to ensure acquittal of an innocent but to thwart that very system."[26]

Obama caved to the conservative pressure. The administration delayed closure of Guantanamo; it announced plans to try some civilian detainees in military tribunals and give others no trial at all.[27] The administration banned the army from using torture but exempted the CIA. The administration refused to repudiate extraordinary rendition or prosecute members of the Bush administration responsible for gross violations of the Constitution. Even worse, the Obama administration continued Bush-era policies of aggression overseas. Critics refer to Obama's foreign policy as "Bush lite."

I strongly believe the United States must radically shift gears. It must recognize the difference between isolated fanatics and groups fighting for legitimate causes, even if we disagree with their ideology and tactics. It must pull out all U.S. troops and mercenaries from Iraq, Afghanistan, and Pakistan. It must take immediate steps to resolve the Israeli-Palestinian issue. Such a shift in policy will do more to undermine groups such as al Qaeda than all U.S. invasions combined.

Like the communist menace of years past, the terrorist menace is used to terrify people into accepting aggression abroad and repression at home. Ironically, the phony war against communism had an actual end, the collapse of the Soviet Union. The Global War on Terrorism has no end. I don't think, however, that the American people will accept perpetual war, thousands of deaths, and the waste of trillions of dollars. At some point an American administration will simply drop the disastrous policy. I hope that day comes very soon.

GWOT will end, not in victory, but with a whimper.

Afterword:
Terrorism and Empire

On the day of 9/11, I was at home. Someone called and I turned on the radio. It was plainly a horrendous act of terror. In my first interviews, I made the pretty obvious point that power systems all over the world would exploit the fear engendered for their own ends: escalating aggression and repression, and controlling their own populations. The United States was no exception. Many of these efforts succeeded.

If the goal had been to reduce terror, the United States would have used the ample opportunity to make use of the fact that core elements of the jihadi movement were bitterly critical of the terrorist crime. Such an approach would have isolated al Qaeda instead of mobilizing support for bin Laden. By supporting his claims about a Western war against Islam, the United State became his best ally, in the phrase of Michael Scheuer, the chief CIA operative tracking bin Laden for many years. The highly respected U.S. interrogator Matthew Alexander spelled out how the Cheney-Rumsfeld torture regime also created terrorists and mobilized others to the cause, probably killing more American soldiers than the toll of 9/11, in his estimation. The Torture Memos reveal that Cheney-Rumsfeld kept calling for harsher measures to try to elicit information to show that Saddam was linked to bin Laden, a needed pretext for the Iraq invasion.

Al Qaeda is described by specialists as a loose network of networks, which seeks to be a vanguard, mobilizing aggrieved populations to its cause by spectacular actions. The threat is real, and there
are ways to reduce it, among them what I just mentioned, but in many
other ways as well. But these ways were not considered. It is not that
the Bush administration preferred terror. Rather, preventing it was
not high on the list of priorities.

Terrorism is a crime, and should be treated as such: identify the
perpetrators, apprehend them, and give them fair trials. Beyond that
it is necessary to attend to the grievances that regularly lie in the background of terrorism, and when they are legitimate, remedy them—
which should be done anyway. And it is necessary to convince the
pool of potential recruits that there is a better course. That's the right
approach if the aim is to reduce terrorism. And it works. Indonesia
and Northern Ireland are good examples.

I have been writing about terrorism ever since the Reagan administration declared its "War on Terror" in 1981. I have been using the
official United States and British government definitions, which seem
to me accurate enough (see chapter 1). But that definition is unac-
ceptable, because it follows at once that the United States is a leading
terrorist state. Accordingly, it has been necessary to craft some new
definition that will restrict "terror" to what *they* do to *us*, excluding
what *we* do to *them*. That is a difficult task. The norm is to overlook
the problem and just disregard our own terrorism and that of our
clients. There's nothing subtle about it.

The contrived War on Terrorism is just the latest excuse for
expanding the system of global domination. George Washington
described the United States as an "infant empire," and the Founding
Fathers had an expansive vision. For Jefferson, the colonies would
be the "nest" from which the whole hemisphere would be peopled,
replacing Red and Black and Latin. Other similar visions were shaped
as circumstances allowed.

Inculcating fear is a standard method adopted by power systems to control populations, almost reflexively. Thus Hitler had to invade Poland to defend peaceful Germany from the "wild terror" of the Poles. And so on through history. How it is done depends on specific cultural, social, and historical circumstances.

The United States has been an unusually frightened society since colonial days. One of the best studies of these matters is by literary critic H. Bruce Franklin in *War Stars: The Superweapon and the American Imagination*. He surveys popular media back to the earliest days and finds some striking and persistent themes. One is fear that some awesome enemy is about to overwhelm us, and we are saved at the last minute by a super weapon or superhero (with variants). Another theme is that the enemy commonly turns out to be our victims: Native Americans, blacks, Chinese immigrants, etcetera. Leaders can play on these fears, and do.

Fear of communism took many forms. In the pre–World War II period, the United States supported Mussolini, and to an extent Hitler, because they were holding the line against the working classes ("communists"). During World War II Stalin became the lovable "Uncle Joe." Later he was about to lead the Russian hordes to overwhelm us, though the Yellow Chinese were even more threatening. The war on terror was declared by Reagan in 1981, as the communist threat was becoming less credible.

No one laughed when Reagan put on his John Wayne act and called a national emergency because the dread army of Nicaragua was only two days from Harlingen, Texas, or when imaginary Libyan hit men were lurking in the streets of Washington to assassinate Our Leader, or when the nutmeg capital of the world (Grenada) was building a tourist airbase that the Russians might use to bomb us (if they could find it on a map).

After the fall of the Berlin wall, and the Russians weren't coming anymore, the Bush I administration presented a new National Security Strategy and budget. They essentially declared that everything would proceed as before, but with new pretexts. Thus we needed a huge military system because of the "technological sophistication" of third world powers. We had to maintain intervention forces aimed at the oil-producing regions of the Middle East, where the serious threats to our interest could not be laid at the Kremlin's door, contrary to decades of deceit.

Shortly thereafter, Reagan-Bush's close friend Saddam Hussein disobeyed orders, invaded Kuwait in 1990, and instantly became the reincarnation of Hitler. In 2002, when the United States was planning to invade Iraq, Americans were warned of mushroom clouds over New York. And so it proceeds as circumstances change. The threats are often real, though it is easy to show that defense against these threats is rarely a high priority, and actions are often taken that consciously increase the threats because priorities lie elsewhere.

The major media contribute to the misinformation propagated by governments, not only in the United States. They commonly adopt the general perspective of systems of power, both state and private. The War on Terrorism is no exception.

Journalism at its best is a noble cause, bringing to the general population insights and truths about the world that systems of power seek to conceal and distort in their own interests. Honest journalism is a hard road to follow, perhaps even more so than honest scholarship. But it can be done, as *Conversations with Terrorists* illustrates. Through firsthand reporting from conflict zones around the Middle East, Erlich provides an excellent account not usually seen in the mainstream media.

Noam Chomsky
March 18, 2010

Notes

CHAPTER 1

1. The Taliban criticized the 9/11 attacks, as did Muslim leaders around the world. Recently declassified U.S. government documents indicate that Mullah Omar may not have been aware of the 9/11 planning done by Osama bin Laden, something both he and bin Laden have said for many years. See Gareth Porter, "Taliban Regimes Pressed Bin Laden on anti-U.S. Terror," Inter Press Service, February 12, 2009, www.ipsnews.net/news.asp?idnews =50300.

2. In September 2001, the Senate and House passed a joint resolution called the "Authorization for Use of Military Force Against Terrorists." It authorizes the President to use military force against anyone responsible for the 9/11 attacks. Administrations have used the authorization as a legal excuse to attack alleged terrorists anywhere in the world, even those with no connection to 9/11.

3. A. G. Sulzberger, "Cheney Says Obama Has Increased Risks," *New York Times*, March 15, 2009.

4. Executive Order 13224, Office of the Coordinator for Counterterrorism, U.S. Department of State, September 23, 2001, www.treasury.gov/offices/enforcement/ofac/programs/terror/terror.pdf.

5. David Cesarani, "Remember Cable Street? Wrong Battle, Mate," *History and Policy*, www.historyandpolicy.org/papers/policy-paper-93.html.

6. Henry Grumwald, "An Interview with Hafez Assad," *Time*, June 21, 2005, www.time.com/time/magazine/article/0,9171,1075212,00.html. See also Sam Housseini, "International Law Won't Shield Libyan Agents; Air

Hijacking," letter to the editor, *New York Times*, March 3, 1992, www.ny times.com/1992/03/03/opinion/l-international-law-won-t-shield-libyan -agents-air-hijacking-791092.html?scp=1&sq=1954%20Israel%20hijacks %20Syrian%20plane&st=cse&pagewanted=print.

7. Mike Davis, "A History of the Car Bomb," *Asia Times*, April 13, 2006, http://atimes.com/atimes/Front_Page/HD13Aa01.html.

8. Stephen Kinzer, *All the Shah's Men: An American Coup and the Roots of Middle East Terror* (New York: John Wiley and Sons, 2003), 1–16.

9. Reese Erlich, *Dateline Havana: The Real Story of U.S. Policy and the Future of Cuba* (Sausalito: Polipoint Press, 2009), 21–27.

10. Quoted in Noam Chomsky, "International Terrorism: Image and Reality," in *Western State Terrorism*, ed. Alexander George (London: Routledge, 1991), www.chomsky.info/articles/199112--02.htm.

11. Rachel Donadio, "Judge Links Italy Agency to Abduction of a Cleric," *New York Times*, January 2, 2010.

12. Prince Norodom Sihanouk was the neutralist leader of Cambodia who opposed the U.S. war against Vietnam. In 1970, the United States instigated a coup against Sihanouk and installed a military dictator. This paved the way for a massive U.S. bombing campaign and invasion of Cambodia, which turned Cambodians decisively against the United States and led to the Khmer Rouge coming to power. The Khmer Rouge was an ultra-left communist party responsible for the deaths of over a million Cambodians until it was overthrown in 1978.

13. The United States justified its fight against communism on the grounds that the Soviet Union and/or China could invade and occupy the United States or U.S. allies in Europe and Asia. In reality, the Soviet Union and China never realistically posed such a threat. The Soviet Union preferred to challenge U.S. hegemony by supporting governments and movements in the third world, and to a lesser degree, supporting leftist parties seeking electoral victory in Europe. The Soviet Union had its own hegemonistic policies that led it to keep troops stationed in Eastern Europe and invade Afghanistan. But the United States needed a much bigger boogie man, and created the myth of communist world domination.

14. "U.S. Defense Outlays by Function and Subfunction, 1962–2014," U.S. Government chart of military budgets, www.whitehouse.gov/omb/ budget/fy2010/assets/hist03z2.xls.

15. Anup Shah, "World Military Spending," *Global Issues*, September 9, 2009. See chart "U.S. Military Spending vs. the World, 2008," www.global issues.org/article/75/world-military-spending#InContextUSMilitary SpendingVersusRestoftheWorld.

16. Chalmers Johnson, *Nemesis: The Last Days of the American Republic*

(New York: Holt Books, 2008), excerpted in www.globalresearch.ca/index .php?context=va&aid=12824.

17. President Jimmy Carter, State of the Union Address, January 23, 1980.

18. Iraq's Saddam Hussein illegally invaded and occupied Kuwait. But the United States never seriously pursued diplomatic means to end that occupation. The first Gulf War gave the United States an opportunity to expand its economic and military power in the region.

19. Jane Perlez, "Deaths of 3 G.I.'s in Pakistan Show Low-Key U.S. Role," *New York Times*, February 4, 2010.

20. Mark Mazzetti and Jane Perlez, "C.I.A. Bolsters Pakistan Spies with Wary Eye," *New York Times,* February 25, 2010.

21. Sabrina Tavernise, "Study Finds 3,000 Pakistanis Were Killed in '09 Militant Attacks," *New York Times*, January 14, 2010, www.nytimes.com/ 2010/01/14/world/asia/14pstan.html.

22. "Pakistani Public Opinion: Growing Concerns about Extremism, Continuing Discontent with U.S.," Pew Global Attitudes Project, August 13, 2009, http://pewglobal.org/reports/pdf/265.pdf.

23. *Small Arms Survey 2009*, Graduate School of International and Development Studies in Geneva, www.smallarmssurvey.org/files/sas/ publications/yearb2003.html.

24. "49 Civilians Killed in Air Strike: Local Yemeni Official," Agence France Press, December 20, 2009, http://ca.news.yahoo.com/s/afp/091220/ world/yemen_unrest_qaeda; Thom Shanker and Mark Landler, "U.S. Aids Yemeni Raids on Al Qaeda, Officials Say," *New York Times*, December 19, 2009, www.nytimes.com/2009/12/19/world/middleeast/19yemen.html ?_r=1&pagewanted=print.

25. M.K. Bhadrakumar, "Obama's Yemeni Odyssey Targets China," *Asia Times*, January 9, 2010, www.atimes.com/atimes/Middle_East/LA09Ak02 .html.

26. "Interview: Anwar al-Awlaki," *Al Jazeera* online, February 7, 2010, http://english.aljazeera.net/focus/2010/02/2010271074776870.htm.

CHAPTER 2

1. The Stern Gang and the Irgun, two right-wing Israeli groups, assassinated British officials and murdered Arab civilians in terrorist bombings. Two of their leaders later became Israeli prime ministers: Menachem Begin and Yitzhak Shamir. See chapter 3.

2. Khaled Meshal, interview with author, Damascus, December 18, 2008. In June 2006, Hamas and the Palestinian Authority (PA) signed an agreement calling for establishment of a Palestinian state in the territory

occupied by Israel in the 1967 war, with its capital in Jerusalem. Although Hamas does not hold that position, it has agreed to follow previous agreements reached by the PA. Meshal met with former president Jimmy Carter and expressed sentiments similar to those expressed in my meeting. See Ethan Bronner, "Carter Says Hamas and Syria Are Open to Peace," *New York Times*, April 22, 2008, www.nytimes.com/2008/04/22/world/middle east/22mideast.html?_r=2#

For a complete explanation of the Hamas-PA agreement, see "Highlights of Hamas-Fatah agreement," *Boston Globe*, June 28, 2006, www.boston.com/news/world/middleeast/articles/2006/06/28/highlights_of_hamas_fatah _agreement.

3. Reese Erlich and Peter Coyote, "The Murders at Al-Sukariya," *Vanity Fair* online, October 22, 2009, www.vanityfair.com/politics/features/2009/10/al-sukariya-200910.

4. Khaled Qadomi, interview with author, Damascus, December 18, 2009.

5. Although disputed by Israel, the international community has reached a consensus on resolving the Israeli-Palestinian issue. According to numerous UN resolutions and a 2002 peace proposal by the Arab League, Israel must withdraw from Syria's Golan Heights and the West Bank. It must recognize a viable, contiguous Palestinian state in Gaza and the West Bank with East Jerusalem as its capital, and must resolve the issue of exiled Palestinians (the right of return). Exact details would be negotiated between Israeli and Palestinian leaders. If Israel meets these conditions, Palestine and surrounding Arab countries would extend diplomatic recognition and live in peace with Israel. For the text of the 2002 Arab League proposal, see http://news .bbc.co.uk/2/hi/world/monitoring/media_reports/1899395.stm.

6. Meshal, interview December 18, 2008. In other interviews Meshal has expressed support for a 10-year ceasefire with Israel and a willingness to live with a two-state solution. See BBC interview, February 8, 2006, news.bbc.co .uk/go/pr/fr/-/2/hi/middle_east/4693382.stm.

7. "The Covenant of the Islamic Resistance Movement (Hamas)," Article 27, August 18, 1988, http://avalon.law.yale.edu/20th_century/hamas.asp.

8. Ibid., Article 11.

9. Lechi, also known as the Stern Gang, explicitly called for Israel to expand from the Nile to the Euphrates (see chapter 3). Today's right-wing Zionists claim each successive territory conquered by Israel (Egyptian Sinai, Gaza, West Bank, Syria's Golan Heights, south Lebanon) is Jewish land because they had been part of ancient Israel.

10. The Israeli government and its supporters try to equate all criticism of Israel or Zionism with anti-Semitism. Prior to 1948, most Jews did not consider themselves Zionists, and today, some Jewish critics of Israel

continue to oppose Zionism as an ideology. Some ultra-Orthodox Jews also reject Zionism for religious reasons.

11. "The Covenant of the Islamic Resistance Movement," Article 7.

12. "The Protocols of the Elders of Zion" first appeared in Russia in 1903, purportedly written by a secret Jewish organization bent on world domination through control of banks and media. In reality, it was a forged document used as anti-Jewish propaganda by the Russian Secret Police and aristocrats.

13. "The Covenant of the Islamic Resistance Movement," Article 22.

14. "Ever since they occupied Gaza, the Israelis had been cultivating Yassin, a Muslim Brother who'd be jailed by Egypt—in their struggle against Palestinian nationalism, much as the Americans had supported the Afghan mujahedin" in Afghanistan. Adam Shatz, "Mishal's Luck," *London Review of Books*, May 14, 2009.

15. Although Israeli leaders condemned the Baruch Goldstein massacre, he remains a hero to some Israelis. Those Zionists made pilgrimages to his gravesite in the settlement of Kiryat Arba, near Hebron, until the Israeli government tore down the shrine and prayer area in 1999.

16. In 2001, the Popular Front for the Liberation of Palestine (PFLP) assassinated ultra-right-wing Israeli cabinet minister Rechavam Zeevi in a Jerusalem hotel. The Israeli government denounced the assassination as terrorism; the PFLP said it had legitimately killed a wartime leader.

17. For the best account of the assassination attempt, see Paul McGeough, *Kill Khaled: The Failed Mossad Assassination of Khaled Meshal and the Rise of Hamas* (New York: New Press, 2009).

18. Nicolas Pelham and Max Rodenbeck, "Which Way for Hamas?" *New York Review of Books*, November 5, 2009.

19. When the Israeli army seized the West Bank and Gaza in 1967, the government said it would return the land in exchange for peace with Arab countries. But both labor and conservative Israeli governments subsequently built settlements in the occupied territories in contravention of international law. The settlements remain the largest stumbling block to a peace plan. Statistics on the growth of the settlements can be found at "Comprehensive Settlement Population 1972–2008," Foundation for Middle East Peace. Source: Israeli Central Bureau of Statistics, www.fmep.org/settlement_info/settlement-info-and-tables/stats-data/comprehensive-settlement-population-1972-2006.

20. Official observers from Britain, the European Union, and the United States all declared the elections free and fair. See, for example, the Carter Center report, www.cartercenter.org/news/multimedia/PeacePrograms/PalestinianElectionObservation2006.html.

21. Khaled Meshal, "We Will Not Sell Our People or Principles for Foreign Aid," *Guardian* (London), op-ed, January 31, 2006, www.guardian.co.uk/world/2006/jan/31/comment.israelandthepalestinians.

22. *Human Rights In Palestine and Other Occupied Arab Territories: Report of the United Nations Fact Finding Mission on the Gaza Conflict* (The Goldstone Report), September 15, 2009, 22, http://image.guardian.co.uk/sys-files/Guardian/documents/2009/09/15/UNFFMGCReport.pdf. Israeli officials refused to meet with the UN Mission and predictably denounced the report's findings. They even tried to claim that Goldstone, a Jew who opposed apartheid and headed up numerous human rights investigations in other countries, is somehow "anti-Semitic." The Goldstone Report criticized war crimes by both sides but emphasized the disproportionate violations by the IDF.

23. Ibid., 24.

24. Ibid., 32–33.

25. Katherine Butler, foreign editor, "Explainer: Israel's Attack on Gaza," *Independent* (London), December. 29, 2008, www.independent.co.uk/news/world/middle-east/explainer-israels-attack-on-gaza-1215044.html.

26. Israel also claimed victory over Hezbollah in the July 2006 invasion of Lebanon, but much of the world considered Hezbollah the victor. Hezbollah had some major military successes, including the first sinking of an Israeli navy destroyer. Hezbollah's domestic support shot up after the war while Israeli leaders squabbled and blamed each other for failures during the war. The war contributed to the resignation of Prime Minister Ehud Olmert. See Reese Erlich, *The Iran Agenda: The Real Story of U.S. Policy and the Middle East Crisis* (Sausalito: Polipoint Press, 2007), 45–50.

27. Goldstone Report, 21.

28. Ibid., 23.

29. "Hamas: Amnesty Report Accusing Us of War Crimes Is 'Unfair,'" *Haaretz* (Tel Aviv), February 7, 2009, www.haaretz.com/hasen/spages/1097267.html.

30. Sheera Frenkel, "UN to Accept $10m in Compensation from Israel for Gaza War Damage," *Times* (London), January 9, 2010, www.timesonline.co.uk/tol/news/world/middle_east/article6981539.ece.

31. Stephen Farrell and Nicholas Blanford, "Who Controls Hamas—Haniya or Mashaal?" *Times* (London), July 10, 2006, www.timesonline.co.uk/tol/news/world/middle_east/article685619.ece.

32. Meshal, *Guardian*, January 31, 2006.

33. Fawaz A. Gerges, "Hamas Is a Mideast Reality," *Los Angeles Times*, op-ed, January 31, 2009, http://articles.latimes.com/2009/jan/31/opinion/oe-gerges31.

34. About 20 percent of Israeli citizens are of Palestinian origin (Israeli

Arabs). Many live in poverty and have few political rights compared with Israeli Jews. Israeli leaders have always distrusted Arabs living in Israel and see them as potential fifth columnists. All Palestinian groups call for the return of refugees forced to flee the wars of 1948 and 1967. Hard-line Palestinians insist that the refugees be allowed to return to their homes anywhere in Israel. The PLO accepted the concept that the vast majority of Palestinians would return to an independent Palestinian state and/or accept monetary compensation for their property lost years ago. Thus Israel would remain a majority Jewish in practice but without a formal acceptance by Palestinian leaders.

35. Hamas's Arabic language website is www.diwan.ps.

36. Shariah is a legal system based on Islamic teachings. Each country interprets it differently. The Philippines allows Muslims to apply Shariah only to family law. Saudi Arabian Shariah allows authorities to cut off the hands of thieves and behead adulterers.

37. Taghreed El-Khodary and Ethan Bronner, "Hamas Fights, Often Within Its Ranks, Over Gaza's Islamist Identity," *New York Times*, September 6, 2009.

38. Palestinian Centre for Human Rights, press release, August 15, 2009, www.pchrgaza.org/files/PressR/English/2009/press2009.html.

39. Nicolas Pelham and Max Rodenbeck, "Which Way for Hamas?" *New York Review of Books*, November 5, 2009, www.nybooks.com/articles/23313?utm_source=feedburner&utm_medium=feed&utm_campaign=feed%3a+nybooks+(the+new+york+review+of+books).

40. "Under Cover of War," Human Rights Watch, April, 19, 2009, www.hrw.org/en/node/82359/section/2.

41. The same Human Rights Watch Report also strongly criticizes Fatah for similar crimes against Hamas supporters living in the West Bank.

42. Ethan Bronner, "Olmert Says Israel Should Pull Out of West Bank," *New York Times*, September 30, 2008.

43. Shawan Jabarin, interview with author, Ramallah, West Bank, November 5, 2009.

CHAPTER 3

1. Ronny Perlman, interview with author, Jerusalem, November 6, 2009.

2. Mustafa Barghouthi, interview with author, Ramallah, November 4, 2009.

3. Geula Cohen, *Woman of Violence: Memoirs of a Young Terrorist* (New York: Holt, Rinehart & Winston, 1966), 7.

4. Ibid., 18.

5. Geula Cohen, interview with author, Jerusalem, November 6, 2009.

6. Yair Stern, interview with author, Jerusalem, November 4, 2009.

7. Cohen, *Woman of Violence*, 24.

8. Sylvain Cypel, *Walled: Israeli Society at an Impasse* (New York: Other Press, 2006), 116.

9. Larry Collins and Dominique Lapierre, *O Jerusalem* (New York: Simon and Shuster Paperbacks, 1972), 137.

10. Ibid., 133.

11. Cohen interview, November 6, 2009.

12. Cohen, *Woman of Violence*, 55.

13. Simha Flapan, *Zionism and the Palestinians* (London: Croom and Helm, 1979), 141–42.

14. Collins and La Pierre, *O Jerusalem*, 193–95.

15. Ibid., 207–9.

16. Uri Avnery, "The Israeli-Arab War of 1948," October 5, 2008, www .israelpalestina.info/modules.php?name=News&file=article&sid=778.

17. UN Special Committee on Palestine, press release, August 31, 1947, www.mideastweb.org/unscop1947.htm.

18. Ibid.

19. Alan Hart, *Arafat: Terrorist or Peacemaker?* (London: Sidgwick & Jackson, 1984), 53.

20. Cohen interview, November 6, 2009.

21. Collins and Lapierre, *O Jerusalem,* 276.

22. Hart, *Arafat*, 56.

23. Cohen interview, November 6, 2009.

24. Geula Cohen, interview with author, Hebron, June 26, 1987.

25. Shawan Jabarin, interview with author, Ramallah, November 4, 2009.

26. Cohen interview, November 6, 2009.

27. David Wilder, interview with author, Hebron, November 2, 2009.

CHAPTER 4

1. Bush administration neoconservatives hoped that the U.S. invasion of Iraq would lead to the overthrow of governments in Iran and Syria as well. As we see later in this chapter, President al-Assad is convinced that Bush was trying to overthrow him.

2. In 2008 the Bush administration removed North Korea from the list of state sponsors of terrorism, although North Korean leaders made no actual changes in policy toward terrorism. See Reese Erlich, *Dateline Havana: The Real Story of U.S. Policy and the Future of Cuba* (Sausalito: Polipoint Press, 2009), 196–97.

3. Bashar al-Assad, interview with author, Damascus, June 11, 2006.

4. Seymour Hersh, "The Syrian Bet," *New Yorker*, July 28, 2003, www .newyorker.com/archive/2003/07/28/030728fa_fact?printable=true.

5. On October 12, 2000, suicide bombers blew up the Navy's USS *Cole*, docked in Aden, Yemen. The U.S. accused al Qaeda of carrying out the attack in which 17 sailors died and 39 were injured.

6. Maher Arar, CBC News online, November 4, 2003, www.cbc.ca/ news/background/arar/arar_statement.html.

7. Commission of Inquiry into the Actions of Canadian Officials in Relation to Maher Arar (Arar Commission), Canadian Government Publishing, 2006, www.fedpubs.com/subject/govern/arar.htm.

8. Al-Assad interview, June 11, 2006.

9. U.S. State Department, Office of the Coordinator for Counterterrorism, *Country Reports on Terrorism 2008*, chapter 3, "State Sponsors of Terrorism," April 30, 2009, www.state.gov/s/ct/rls/crt/2008/122436.htm.

10. The 1978 Camp David Accords were signed between Israel and Egypt. Israel returned the occupied Sinai to Egypt, which in turn diplomatically recognized Israel. The 1993 Oslo Accords were signed between Israel and the PLO. Both sides agreed to complete negotiations within five years to establish an independent Palestinian state in Gaza and the West Bank, but the accords were never fully implemented.

11. Al-Assad interview, June 11, 2006.

12. Bashar al-Assad, interview with author, Damascus, June 14, 2006.

13. "Syria's Quneitra Hoax," Committee for Accuracy in Middle East Reporting in America (CAMERA), May 10, 2001, www.camera.org/index .asp?x_context=3&x_outlet=14&x_article=49.

14. Mohammad Ali, interview with author, June 7, 2006.

15. "A Question Mark Over the Death of a City," *Times* (London), February 17, 1975.

16. UN General Assembly Resolution 3240, November, 29, 1974, www .jewishvirtuallibrary.org/jsource/UN/unga31_106.html.

17. Contrary to myths spread by the Bush administration, Osama bin Laden's al Qaeda had no political or military ties to Saddam Hussein's government in Iraq. The two hated one another. But after the U.S. invasion, Sunni fundamentalists flocked to Iraq to make jihad against the foreign occupier. Al Qaeda in Iraq is a home-grown insurgent group with few operational ties to Osama bin Laden. In fact, bin Laden criticized the group for its suicide bombings of Iraqi civilians.

18. For many years hawkish Republicans and Democrats denounced efforts to set timetables for a withdrawal of U.S. troops from Iraq. However, faced with mounting pressure from all sectors of Iraqi society, and the war's unpopularity at home, the Bush administration was forced to sign the Status

of Forces Agreement that not only set timetables for reducing troop levels but also set a legally binding withdrawal date. However, the Obama administration may employ the old "I had my fingers crossed" defense to argue that conditions have changed, and U.S. troops must remain after 2011. As of this writing, the United States is hoping to leave 50,000 troops in Iraq after the 2011 deadline, supposedly to train Iraqi soldiers.

19. U.S. State Department, *Country Reports on Terrorism*.

20. Al-Assad interview, June 11, 2006.

21. Robert Burns, "Patraeus: Syria May Slow Iraq Fighters," *Washington Post*, April 27, 2007.

22. Portions of the section on al-Sukariya originally appeared in Reese Erlich and Peter Coyote, "Murders at Al-Sukariya," *Vanity Fair* online, October 26, 2009, www.vanityfair.com/politics/features/2009/10/al-sukariya-200910.

23. Sheik Nawaf al-Bashir, interview with author, Syria, June 12, 2006.

24. "UN Finds New Clues in Hariri Case," BBC News, December 3, 2008, http://news.bbc.co.uk/go/pr/fr/-/2/hi/middle_east/7761919.stm.

25. Ingrid Burke, "UN Lebanon Tribunal Orders Release of 4 Generals Accused in Hariri Assassination," *Jurist*, April 29, 2009, http://jurist.law.pitt.edu/paperchase/2009/04/un-lebanon-tribunal-orders-release-of-4.php.

26. Prior to 1990, Syria had close ties with the USSR and Eastern Europe, from whom it received political, economic, and military backing. As the Soviet Union was collapsing, however, Hafez al-Assad changed camps and briefly allied with the United States.

27. Al-Assad interview, June 11, 2006.

28. Human Rights Watch, "No Room to Breathe: State Repression of Human Rights Activism in Syria," October 2007, www.hrw.org/sites/default/files/reports/syria1007.pdf.

29. Amnesty International Report 2009, "Syria," www.report2009.amnesty.org/en/regions/middle-east-north-africa/syria.

30. Al-Assad interview, June 14, 2006. For more information about the Beirut-Damascus declaration, see www.free-syria.com/en/loadarticle.php?articleid=6924.

31. Holly Fletcher, "State Sponsor: Syria," Council on Foreign Relations, February 2008, www.cfr.org/publication/9368/.

CHAPTER 5

1. On October 23, 1983, suicide bombers drove trucks into barracks occupied by French and American soldiers then occupying Lebanon. The bombs killed 299 soldiers, including 241 U.S. Marines. The United States

and France called the attack a horrendous act of terrorism. Most Lebanese saw it as a legitimate military tactic against foreign occupiers. The attack was a crucial turning point in the conflict. The Reagan administration withdrew U.S. troops from Lebanon in February 1984, a decision that exposes the myth that the United States "never gives in to terrorism."

2. Bob Woodward, *Veil: The Secret Wars of the CIA 1981-1987* (New York: Simon and Shuster, 1984), 396-97.

3. Ayatollah Mohammad Fadlallah, interview with author, Beirut, December 22, 2008.

CIA Chief Casey also told Woodward that he had later given Fadlallah $2 million in cash for charitable work in exchange for ceasing anti-U.S. activities. Fadlallah denies it. Several more assassination attempts were made against Fadlallah, which suggest the United States either didn't give the money or was unhappy with the results.

4. Ali Jaber, "Beirut Faction Says It Foiled Attack on Leader," *New York Times*, December 10, 1989, www.nytimes.com/1989/12/10/world/beirut -faction-says-it-foiled-attack-on-leader.html?scp=6&sq=fadllah%20 assassination&st=cse&pagewanted=print.

5. Walid Jumblatt, interview with author, Beirut, December 22, 2008.

6. Iran's Ayatollah Khomeini espoused a theory called "velayat-e faqih" or guardianship of the clerics, in which Shia Muslim clerics would become political rulers. This theory served as the basis for the current religious dictatorship in Iran and also gained support among some Shiites in Lebanon.

7. The U.S. government labels all Muslims engaged in armed actions against the United States as terrorists. U.S. officials are well aware of the sometimes extreme differences between the groups but lumps them together for propaganda purposes. See Norman Solomon and Reese Erlich, *Target Iraq: What the News Media Didn't Tell You* (New York: Context Books, 2003), 44.

8. "The Hizballah Program," *Jerusalem Quarterly* 48, Fall 1988, www .ıotandwithuo.com/pdfɛ/flyerɛ/hezbollah_program pdf

9. U.S., French, and Italian troops had originally come to Lebanon as part of a multinational force to evacuate the PLO. They stayed, however, and sided with the Christian Phalangists and other right-wing parties fighting in the country's civil war. Lebanese came to see the Western troops as occupiers.

10. Hala Jaber, *Hezbollah: Born with a Vengeance* (New York: Columbia University Press, 1997), 82-83.

11. "Timeline of Hezbollah Violence," Committee for Accuracy in Middle East Reporting in America (CAMERA), July 17, 2006, www.camera .org/index.asp?x_context=2&x_outlet=118&x_article=1148. CAMERA, a

conservative and pro-Israel Web site, lists examples of terrorism it says were carried out by Hezbollah.

12. The chador is a large semicircle of cloth wrapped around a woman's head and body. It is most often seen in Iran, but is also worn by Shia women throughout the Middle East.

13. Reese Erlich, "A Kinder, Gentler Hezbollah," *San Francisco Bay Guardian*, September 2, 1998.

14. Sheik Nabil Kaouk, interview with author, south Lebanon, August 1, 1998.

15. Ali Hammad Salman, interview with author, south Lebanon, August 1, 1998.

16. Top of Form "Lebanon: The Many Hands and Faces of Hezbollah," IRIN (UN Office for the Coordination of Humanitarian Affairs), March 29, 2006, www.irinnews.org/Report.aspx?ReportId=26242.

17. Farid el Khazen, interview with author, Beirut, July 30, 1998.

18. Robin Wright, "Inside the Mind of Hezbollah," *Washington Post*, July 16, 2006, www.washingtonpost.com/wp-dyn/content/article/2006/07/14/AR2006071401401.html.

19. All significant Palestinian organizations have agreed to a two-state solution if Israel accepts the international consensus for a peace plan. See chapter 2 and "Highlights of Hamas-Fatah agreement," *Boston Globe*, June 28, 2006, www.boston.com/news/world/middleeast/articles/2006/06/28/highlights_of_hamas_fatah_agreement/.

20. Seymour Hersh, "The Syrian Bet," *New Yorker*, July 28, 2003, www.newyorker.com/archive/2003/07/28/030728fa_fact?printable=true.

21. Mohammad Nayef, interview with author, near Khiam Prison, south Lebanon, June 28, 2003.

22. Amnesty International, "Lebanon: Where Is the Door?—Letter from an Amnesty International Delegation Visiting Khiam Prison in South Lebanon," May 29, 2000, www.amnesty.org/en/library/asset/mde18/008/2000/en/80a5dd6f-df0f-11dd-953e-5fb92c895266/mde180082000en.html.

23. According to Lebanese government statistics, 1,181 Lebanese died in the 34-day invasion. Israel says 120 of its soldiers and 39 civilians died. Israel intentionally used cluster bombs that wouldn't fully detonate, and the bomblets promise to continue to cause injuries to Lebanese civilians for years. For more background on the 2006 war, see Reese Erlich, *The Iran Agenda: The Real Story of U.S. Policy and the Middle East Crisis* (Sausalito: Polipoint Press, 2007), 45–50.

24. Beirut Center for Research and Information Poll, July 29, 2006, www.beirutcenter.info/default.asp?contentid=692&MenuID=46.

25. "Hizbullah Helped Locate Salah Ezzedine," *Daily Star* (Beirut),

September 5, 2009, http://lebanesepress.com/hizbullah-helped-locate-salah
-ezzedine.

26. Robert F. Worth, "Billion-Dollar Pyramid Scheme Rivets Lebanon,"
New York Times, September 16, 2009, www.nytimes.com/2009/09/16/
world/middleeast/16lebanon.html?_r=3&ref=world.

27. Ihsan A Hijazi, "'Happy Ending' Is Seen for Hostages in Beirut,"
New York Times, July 25, 1988.www.nytimes.com/1988/07/25/world/
happy-ending-is-seen-for-hostages-in-beirut.html?scp=2&sq=Ayatollah
%20Fadlallah%201985&st=cse&pagewanted=print.

28. Agence France Presse, September 14, 2001, as quoted in "Islamic
Statements Against Terrorism," www.unc.edu/~kurzman/terror.htm.

29. Ayatollah Mohammad Fadlallah, "The Role of a Woman—Part I,"
Bayyna (Fadlallah's Web site in English), http://english.bayynat.org.lb/
WomenFamily/woman1.htm.

CHAPTER 6

1. Right-wing clerics and government officials want women to wear
scarves covering their entire heads, and the traditional chador, a cloth
wrapped around the body. As a sign of rebellion, many younger women push
the scarf back and wear a manteau, or long coat.

2. Inflation hit a high of 30 percent in 2008 but declined to 7.5 percent
by November 2009, according to the International Monetary Fund (IMF).
"IMF Executive Board Concludes 2009 Article IV Consultation with the
Islamic Republic of Iran," Public Information Notice (PIN) No. 10/24,
February 18, 2010, www.imf.org/external/np/sec/pn/2010/pn1024.htm.

3. In 1953 the CIA organized a coup against the democratically elected
government of Prime Minister Mohammad Mossadegh. The United States
installed a shah (king) with dictatorial powers. A popular revolution
overthrew the shah in 1979. For more background, see Reese Erlich, *The Iran
Agenda: The Real Story of U.S. Policy and the Middle East Crisis* (Sausalito:
Polipoint Press, 2007), 51–72.

4. U.S. State Department, "Country Reports on Terrorism 2008," April
30, 2009, www.state.gov/s/ct/rls/crt/2008/122436.htm.

5. Mohsen Sazegara, phone interview with author, January 12, 2010. In
my opinion the U.S. designation of the Revolutionary Guard as terrorists
was a ploy by the Bush administration to put more pressure on Iran. The
designation is rather hypocritical given the history of U.S. government
terrorist attacks against Iran.

6. Farnaz Fassihi, "Fighting a Regime He Helped Create," *Wall Street
Journal*, December 3, 2009.

7. Muhammad Sahimi is a professor of chemical engineering at the University of Southern California and writes about Iranian affairs for Tehran Bureau, among others.

8. Muhammad Sahimi, email interview with author, January 14, 2010.

9. Mohsen Sazegara, phone interview with author, February 1, 2010.

10. Sazegara, interview, January 12, 2010.

11. Erlich, *The Iran Agenda*, 77–82.

12. "Witness Statement of Mohsen Sazegara," Iran Human Rights Documentation Center, approved by Sazegara on November 10, 2008, www.iranhrdc.org/httpdocs/English/pdfs/WitnessStatements/MSWS.pdf.

13. Golnar Esfandiari, "Iran: Former Revolutionary Mohsen Sazegara Talks About Parting Ways with Theocracy," Radio Farda, February 10, 2007, http://www.rferl.org/content/article/1074612.html.

14. The Washington Institute for Near East Policy was founded by two former members of AIPAC and has included many AIPAC members on its board of directors. Mark H. Milstein, "Washington Institute for Near East Policy: An AIPAC 'Image Problem,'" *Washington Report on Middle East Affairs,* July 1991, www.washington-report.org/backissues/0791/9107030.htm.

15. Muhammad Sahimi, "The Sheikh of Reform: Mehdi Karroubi," Tehran Bureau, www.pbs.org/wgbh/pages/frontline/tehranbureau/2009/10/the-sheikh-of-the-reforms-mehdi-karroubi.html. See also Erlich, *The Iran Agenda*, 86.

16. The Basiji are a paramilitary militia trained and led by the Revolutionary Guard. "Iran: Basij Member Describes Election Abuse," Channel 4 News (London), December 16, 2009, www.channel4.com/news/articles/politics/international_politics/iran+basij+member+describes+election+abuse/3466142.

17. Ali Ansari, Daniel Berman, and Thomas Rintoul, "Preliminary Analysis of the Voting Figures in Iran's 2009 Presidential Election," June 21, 2009, www.chathamhouse.org.uk/files/14234_iranelection0609.pdf.

18. Because of government cover-ups, it's very difficult to know how many Iranians died in street protests and in prisons. As of this writing, it's estimated that over 100 people have died for opposing the election fraud, perhaps more.

19. The NILU is a small, national organization helping worker groups communicate and organize. "Ahmadinejad a Progressive?" Web page of Network of Iranian Labor Unions, downloaded January 22, 2010, http://iranlaborreport.com/Politics/Ahmadinejad.html.

20. Parts of this chapter originally appeared in Reese Erlich, "It's Not a Twitter Revolution in Iran," Reuters news wire, op-ed, June 26, 2009.

21. "Iran: Events of 2009," Human Rights Watch Report, www.hrw.org/en/world-report-2010/iran?.

22. Najmeh Bozorgmehr, "Man in the News: Mir-Hossein Moussavi," *Financial Times* (London), January. 8, 2010, www.ft.com/cms/s/0/a9a43a22-fc91-11de-bc51-00144feab49a.html?nclick_check=1.

23. William O. Beeman, "Iran's Uncertain Future," distributed by New American Media, December 31, 2009, http://wbeeman.blogspot.com/2009/12/william-o-beeman-irans-uncertain-future.html.

24. Robert F. Worth, "Opposition in Iran Meets a Crossroads on Strategy," *New York Times,* February 15, 2010.

25. Homayoun Poorzad is the pseudonym of a labor leader living in Iran. Interview with author, 2010.

26. "Interview transcript: Mehdi Karroubi," *Financial Times* (London), January 27, 2010, www.ft.com/cms/s/0/9cfd2964-0a65-11df-ab4a-00144 feabdc0.html.

27. Robin Wright, "Abdolkarim Soroush: The Goals of Iran's Green Movement," *Christian Science Monitor,* January 7, 2010, www.csmonitor.com/layout/set/print/content/view/print/272413.

28. Nazila Fathi, "In Tehran, Thousands Rally to Back Government," *New York Times,* December 31, 2009.

29. Ansari, Berman, and Rintoul, "Preliminary Analysis of the Voting Figures."

30. Mostafa Hejri, "The Green Movement and Responsibilities That Lie Ahead," PDKI Web site, January 20, 2010, http://pdki.org/articles.php?lang=1&cat_id=9&article_id=2161#.

31. For an analysis of positions taken by various Kurdish groups, see Kaveh Ghoreishi, "The Kurds, June Pres Elections and the Aftermath," op-ed, *Roozonline,* January 16, 2010, www.roozonline.com/english/opinion/opinion-article/article/2010/january/16//the-kurds-june-pres-elections-and-the-aftermath.html.

32. Larry Elder, "Unrest in Iran: The Vindication of George W. Bush," distributed by Creators Syndicate, op-ed, December 31, 2009, www.real clearpolitics.com/articles/2009/12/31/unrest_in_iran_the_vindication_of_george_w_bush_99730.html.

33. Mohsen Sazegara, speech at American Enterprise Institute forum, January 30, 2009, www.aei.org/docLib/the-imam-returned-transcirpt.pdf.

34. I recounted this episode in Sean Penn, Ross Mirkarimi, and Reese Erlich, "How to Help Iran without Meddling," *San Francisco Bay Guardian,* July 21, 2009.

35. "Iranian Public on Current Issues," World Public Opinion Web site, www.worldpublicopinion.org/pipa/pdf/sep09/IranUS_Sep09_rpt.pdf.

The results of any public opinion poll in Iran must be viewed with caution because respondents may be reluctant to express their real views. But on the question of attitudes toward U.S. policy, these finding are consistent with previous polls and sentiments expressed to me over many years.

36. Mohsen Sazegara, phone interview with author, February 1, 2010.

37. The United States prohibits U.S. companies from investing in Iran and pressures European companies to do the same. It has hit various Iranian leaders with "smart sanctions," such as freezing foreign bank accounts and prohibiting foreign travel. But to date the smart sanctions have had little impact, and the broader economic sanctions mainly hurt working people.

38. Quoted in testimony of Trita Parsi, "Statement before House Committee on Oversight and Government Reform," December 15, 2009, www.iranian.com/main/blog/niac/niac-testimony-subcommittee-hearing -iran-sanctions-options.

39. Mohammad Abtahi, interview with author, Tehran, June 7, 2009.

40. "Interview with Mohammad Ali Abtahi," PBS Frontline, July 29, 2007, www.pbs.org/wgbh/pages/frontline/showdown/interviews/abtahi .html.

41. "Top Iran Reformist Tells Trial Ahmadinejad Win Was Clean," *Al Manar* (newspaper), August 1, 2009, http://realisticbird.wordpress.com/2009/ 08/01/in-iran-court-abtahi-disputes-vote-fraud-claims-and-trials-begin/.

42. Reese Erlich, "Brad Pitt and the Girl Guerrillas," *Mother Jones*, March/April 2007, http://motherjones.com/politics/2007/03/brad-pitt -and-girl-guerrillas.

43. Under General Director Mohamed ElBaradei, the IAEA consistently criticized Iran for not cooperating fully with the UN but never accused it of having a nuclear weapons program. Yukiya Amano, the general director who began on December 1, 2009, seems more favorable to the U.S. position on Iran. However, as of this writing, the IAEA has not found proof of an Iranian nuclear weapons program. A collection of relevant IAEA reports on Iran can be found at www.iaea.org/NewsCenter/Focus/IaeaIran/index .shtml.

44. "Iran: Nuclear Intentions and Capabilities," National Intelligence Estimate, U.S. Government, December 3, 2007, www.dni.gov/press_ releases/20071203_release.pdf.

45. Erlich, *The Iran Agenda*, 17–34.

46. Nicholas Kulish and Thom Shanker, "West Rejects Iran's Claim That Nuclear Deal Is Near," *New York Times*, February 7, 2010.

47. Chip Cummins, "Caterpillar Prohibits Iran Sales," *Wall Street Journal*, March 2, 2010.

48. Sazegara, phone interview, February 1, 2010.

CHAPTER 7

1. For example, General Abdul Rashid Dostum fought with the pro-Soviet government starting in 1979. He switched sides to join the mujahedeen in the 1980s. He served as President Hamid Karzai's deputy defense minister, was later forced into exile, and—as of this writing—is back in Karzai's good graces.

2. Mullah Mohammad Nizami, interview with author, Kabul, August 26, 2009.

3. Karzai committed massive vote fraud during the 2009 presidential elections, according to UN and other independent election monitors. Karzai surrounds himself with authoritarian warlords, such as Ismail Khan. He was a fundamentalist mujahedeen warlord with the Northern Alliance, the anti-Taliban coalition. After the U.S. invasion, Karzai appointed him governor of Herat Province. Khan refused to turn over national tax money to the central government and used it to build a private army. When Karzai sought to get the money by sending troops to Herat in 2004, Khan fought them with his private militia and 100 people were killed. Khan was later promoted to minister of energy in Kabul.

4. On December 24, 1979, the Soviet Union invaded and occupied Afghanistan to support a pro-Soviet leftist party that had come to power in a coup. The Soviet Union supported a series of reforms, including encouraging women's rights, land reform, and agricultural co-ops. However, Afghans perceived the reforms as being imposed by an occupying power. The CIA, Saudi Arabia, and Pakistan funded and armed those mujahedeen rebels who promoted an extreme, right-wing interpretation of Islam. The increasing repression by Soviet troops and the inability of their allies to govern effectively led to growing resistance and ultimate Soviet withdrawal in 1989. The United States is facing similar difficulties in its war of occupation.

5. Peter L. Bergen, *Holy War, Inc.: Inside the Secret World of Osama bin Laden* (New York: Free Press, 2001), 69.

6. "The CIA's Intervention in Afghanistan; Interview with Zbigniew Brzezinski," *Le Nouvel Observateur*, Paris, January. 15–21, 1998, www .globalresearch.ca/articles/BRZ110A.html.

7. General Shaukat Qadir, interview with author, Rawalpindi, Pakistan, January 3, 2002.

8. Some believe that U.S. officials gave the "blind Sheik" a visa so he could carry out terrorist attacks in the United States. I don't agree. I believe they were rewarding him for services rendered in Afghanistan and didn't anticipate his violent actions. This is an example of opportunistic, self-defeating U.S. foreign policy.

9. "Taliban in Texas for Talks on Gas Pipeline," BBC News, December 4, 1997, http://news.bbc.co.uk/2/hi/world/west_asia/37021.stm.

10. "Powell Announces 43 Million Dollars in New US Aid for Afghans," AFP wire report, May 17, 2001, www.afghan-web.com.

11. Firouz Sedarat, "Bin Laden Urges Europe to Quit Afghanistan," Reuters, November 29, 2007, http://uk.reuters.com/article/idUKL291291 1920071129?pageNumber=2&virtualBrandChannel=0&sp=true.

12. "U.S. Rejects Taliban Offer to Try bin Laden," CNN.com, October 7, 2001, http://archives.cnn.com/2001/US/10/07/ret.us.taliban.

13. Medea Benjamin, interview with author, Kabul, January 17, 2002.

14. "Most Opium Reported Grown in Northern Alliance Areas," UN Wire, October 5, 2001, www.unwire.org/unwire/20011005/19106_story .asp. A UN Report prepared prior to the U.S. invasion noted that whereas the Taliban had drastically reduced opium growing, the Northern Alliance had not done so in areas under its control.

15. Obeidullah Shanawaz, interview with author, Kabul, January 18, 2002.

16. Rick Reyes, interview with author, Kabul, August 30, 2009.

17. Carlotta Gall, "U.S. Killed 90 in Afghan Village, Including 60 Children, U.N. Finds," New York Times, August 27, 2008, www.nytimes .com/2008/08/27/world/asia/27herat.html.

18. Human Rights Watch, "The Human Cost: The Consequences of Insurgent Attacks in Afghanistan," April 15, 2007, www.hrw.org/en/node/ 10984/section/8.

19. Reuel Marc Gerecht, "The Meaning of al Qaeda's Double Agent," Wall Street Journal, op-ed, January 8, 2010.

20. "Afghans Paid $2.5bn in Bribes," BBC News, January 19, 2010, http://news.bbc.co.uk/go/pr/fr/-/2/hi/south_asia/8466915.stm.

21. Curt Tarnoff, "Afghanistan: U.S. Foreign Assistance," Congressional Research Service, July 14, 2009, www.fas.org/sgp/crs/row/R40699.pdf.

22. Rangin Dadfar Spanta, interview with author, Kabul, August 30, 2009. Portions of this chapter first appeared in my article "Aid Often Misses Afghans," San Francisco Chronicle, October 4, 2009, www.sfgate.com/ cgi-bin/article.cgi?f=/c/a/2009/10/04/MN8L19NHRM.DTL.

23. Afzal Rashid, interview with author, Sacramento, August 20, 2009.

24. Lisa Gihring, Chemonics spokesperson, email to author, September 10, 2009.

25. Matt Waldman, Falling Short: Aid Effectiveness in Afghanistan, March 2008, p. 20, www.oxfam.org.uk/resources/policy/debt_aid/downloads/aid _effectiveness_afghanistan.pdf.

26. Jerry Kryschtal, interview with author, Kabul, August 27, 2009.

27. "Taliban Radio Boss Joins Afghan Peace Scheme," Gulf Times

(Dubai), June 11, 2007, www.gulf-times.com/site/topics/printArticle.asp
?cu_no=2&item_no=154449&version=1&template_id=41&parent_id=23.

28. Santwana Dasgupta, interview with author, Kabul, August 27, 2009.

29. After World War II, the United States did help develop the economies of Japan and Europe, reaping tremendous profits for U.S corporations.
But those were industrialized countries with the skilled manpower to recover
relatively quickly. The United States was fighting a cold war with the Soviet
Union and needed those countries as allies. Similarly, South Korea developed in the context of the cold war. Such conditions do not exist today.

30. "Sources: Taliban Split with Al Qaeda, Seek Peace," CNN.com,
October. 6, 2008, http://edition.cnn.com/2008/WORLD/asiapcf/10/06/
afghan.saudi.talks/?iref=mpstoryview.

31. Aryn Baker, "Talking with the Taliban: Easier Said Than Done," *Time*,
November 30, 2009, www.time.com/time/magazine/article/0,9171,1940679,00
.html#ixzz0dBPsMrzw.

32. Eric Schmitt, "Envoy's Cables Show Concerts on War Plans," *New
York Times*, January 26, 2010.

33. David C. Gompert, Terrence K. Kelly, and Jessica Watkins, "Security
in Iraq: A Framework for Analyzing Emerging Threats as U.S. Forces Leave,"
RAND Corporation, www.rand.org/pubs/monographs/2010/RAND_MG
911.sum.pdf. The Bush administration signed a legally binding Status of
Forces Agreement with the government of Iraq promising to remove all troops
and military bases by December 31, 2011. The U.S. government will almost
certainly want to extend its military presence beyond the 2011 deadline, but
the agreement requires Iraqi government consent. Some influential American
think tanks are already advocating continued troop presence.

34. Carlotta Gall, "Rebel Band Presents Peace Plan to Karzai," *New York
Times*, March 24, 2010.

35. Baker, "Talking with the Taliban."

CHAPTER 8

1. Parts of this chapter originally appeared in my article "On the Poppy
Trail," *Progressive*, November 2009.

2. James Risen, "Drug Chieftains Tied to Taliban Are U.S. Targets,"
New York Times, August 10, 2009.

3. Jean Luc Lemahieu, interview with author, Kabul, August 27, 2009.

4. James Risen and Mark Landler, "Accused of Drug Ties, Afghan
Official Worries U.S.," *New York Times,* August 27, 2009, www.nytimes
.com/2009/08/27/world/asia/27kabul.html.

5. Dexter Filkins, Mark Mazzetti, and James Risen, "Brother of Afghan

Leader Said to Be Paid by C.I.A.," *New York Times*, October 28, 2009, www
.nytimes.com/2009/10/28/world/asia/28intel.html?_r=2&hp.

6. Abdoul Waheed Wafa, "Brother of Karzai Denies Links to Heroin,"
New York Times, October 7, 2008.

7. Filkins, Mazzetti, and Risen, "Brother of Afghan Leader."

8. The UNODC issues two reports a year in which it reveals the minimal
role played by the Taliban in the drug trade. But the mainstream media
consistently put a pro-U.S. spin on those reports. For a lengthy critique
of the *New York Times* on this issue, see Jeremy R. Hammond, *"New York
Times* Misleads on Taliban Role in Opium Trade," *Foreign Policy Journal,*
November 29, 2008, www.foreignpolicyjournal.com/2008/11/29/new-york
-times-misleads-on-taliban-role-in-opium-trade.

9. General Shaukat Qadir, interview with author, Rawalpindi, Pakistan,
January 3, 2002.

10. Marcus Walker, Alessandra Migliaccio, and Rick Jervis, "Flood of
Afghan Opium Hits World Markets," *Wall Street Journal,* November 14,
2001.

11. David Rohde, "Taliban Push Poppy Production to a Record Again,"
New York Times, August 26, 2007.

12. Carlotta Gall, "Afghan Poppy Growing Reaches Record Level, U.N.
Says," *New York Times,* November 19, 2004.

13. Pamela Constable, "New Story on How Minister Was Killed/Kabul
Backs Off Conspiracy Charge," *Washington Post*, February 21, 2002, http://
articles.sfgate.com/2002-02-21/news/17531642_1_muslim-pilgrims-foreign
-minister-abdullah-abdullah-interim-leader.

14. James Risen, "Poppy Fields Are Now a Front Line in Afghanistan
War," *New York Times*, May 16, 2007.

15. Norman Solomon and Reese Erlich, *Target Iraq: What the News
Media Didn't Tell You* (New York: Context Books, 2003), 11–20.

16. In 2004 Dan Rather, then anchor of the CBS Evening News and a
correspondent for *60 Minutes,* hosted a story questioning President George
W. Bush's record in the Air National Guard. One document used in the
story was not authentic, but Bush's avoidance of service in Vietnam and long
absence from the National Guard were well-known from other reporting.
Nevertheless, the right wing—backed by the White House—launched a
vicious campaign against CBS and Rather. He left CBS in 2005. Rather sued
CBS for $70 million in damages and reinstatement, and as of this writing,
the suit remains in litigation.

17. "Tax Protester Crashes Plane Into IRS Office," *Wall Street Journal,*
February 19, 2010.

18. Ibid.

19. "Transcript: Senator Lieberman on 'FNS,'" *Fox News*, November 8, 2009, www.foxnews.com/story/0,2933,573056,00.html.

20. "Ahmed Ressam's Millennium Plot," *PBS Frontline*, www.pbs.org/wgbh/pages/frontline/shows/trail/inside/cron.html.

21. Council on American-Islamic Relations, "American Muslims React to Arrest of Algerian in Washington State," press release, December 20, 1999.

22. Hal Benton and Sara Jean Green, "Ressam Judge Decries U.S. Tactics," *Seattle Times*, July 28, 2005, http://seattletimes.nwsource.com/html/localnews/2002406378_ressam27m.html.

23. Henry Weinstein, "Final Two L.A. 8 Defendants Cleared," *Los Angeles Times*, November 1, 2007, http://articles.latimes.com/2007/nov/01/local/me-palestinian1.

24. At first the Obama administration initiated a tactical shift on Iran by emphasizing the need for diplomacy and negotiations. However, after about a year in power, the administration took a more hawkish stand and called for sanctions against Iran that would mainly end up hurting ordinary Iranians. For more details, see chapter 6.

25. Peter Baker, "White House Challenges Terror Critics," *New York Times*, February 8, 2010.

26. Victoria Toensing, "KSM Deserves Military Justice," *Wall Street Journal*, op-ed, March 2, 2010.

27. Jonathan Weisman and Evan Perez, "Obama Leans Towards Switch to Military Trials for 9/11," *Wall Street Journal*, March 6–7, 2010.

Index

About the Author

Reese Erlich's history in journalism goes back 42 years. Today he works as a full-time, freelance print and broadcast reporter, filing for National Public Radio, Market Place Radio, the *San Francisco Chronicle*, and CBC Radio, among other outlets.

Erlich shared a Peabody Award in 2006 as a segment producer for *Crossing East,* a radio documentary on the history of Asians in the United States. He received the Best Depth Reporting award in 2002 from the Society of Professional Journalists (Northern California). His article about the U.S. use of depleted uranium ammunition was voted one of 2003's "most censored stories" by Project Censored at Sonoma State University.

Erlich's book *Target Iraq,* co-authored with Norman Solomon, was a best seller in 2003. *The Iran Agenda: The Real Story of U.S. Policy and the Middle East Crisis* came out in 2007, and *Dateline Havana: The Real Story of U.S. Policy and the Future of Cuba* was released in 2009.

Other Books from PoliPointPress

The Blue Pages: A Directory of Companies Rated by Their Politics and Practices, 2nd edition
Helps consumers match their buying decisions with their political values by listing the political contributions and business practices of over 1,000 companies. $12.95, PAPERBACK.

Sasha Abramsky, *Breadline USA: The Hidden Scandal of American Hunger and How to Fix It*
Treats the increasing food insecurity crisis in America not only as a matter of failed policies, but also as an issue of real human suffering. $23.95, CLOTH.

Rose Aguilar, *Red Highways: A Liberal's Journey into the Heartland*
Challenges red state stereotypes to reveal new strategies for progressives. $15.95, PAPERBACK.

John Amato and David Neiwert, *Over the Cliff: How Obama's Election Drove the American Right Insane*
A witty look at—and an explanation of—the far-right craziness that overtook the conservative movement after Obama became president. $16.95, PAPERBACK.

Dean Baker, *False Profits: Recovering from the Bubble Economy*
Recounts the causes of the economic meltdown and offers a progressive program for rebuilding the economy and reforming the financial system and stimulus programs. $15.95, PAPERBACK.

Dean Baker, *Plunder and Blunder: The Rise and Fall of the Bubble Economy*
Chronicles the growth and collapse of the stock and housing bubbles and explains how policy blunders and greed led to the catastrophic—but completely predictable—market meltdowns. $15.95, PAPERBACK.

Jeff Cohen, *Cable News Confidential: My Misadventures in Corporate Media*
Offers a fast-paced romp through the three major cable news channels—Fox, CNN, and MSNBC—and delivers a serious message about their failure to cover the most urgent issues of the day. $14.95, PAPERBACK.

Marjorie Cohn, *Cowboy Republic: Six Ways the Bush Gang Has Defied the Law*
Shows how the executive branch under President Bush systematically defied the law instead of enforcing it. $14.95, PAPERBACK.

Marjorie Cohn and Kathleen Gilberd, *Rules of Disengagement: The Politics and Honor of Military Dissent*
Examines what U.S. military men and women have done—and what their families and others can do—to resist illegal wars, as well as military racism, sexual harassment, and denial of proper medical care. $14.95, PAPERBACK.

Joe Conason, *The Raw Deal: How the Bush Republicans Plan to Destroy Social Security and the Legacy of the New Deal*
Reveals the well-financed and determined effort to undo the Social Security Act and other New Deal programs. $11.00, PAPERBACK.

Kevin Danaher, Shannon Biggs, and Jason Mark, *Building the Green Economy: Success Stories from the Grassroots*
Shows how community groups, families, and individual citizens have protected their food and water, cleaned up their neighborhoods, and strengthened their local economies. $16.00, PAPERBACK.

Kevin Danaher and Alisa Gravitz, *The Green Festival Reader: Fresh Ideas from Agents of Change*
Collects the best ideas and commentary from some of the most forward green thinkers of our time. $15.95, PAPERBACK.

Reese Erlich, *Dateline Havana: The Real Story of U.S. Policy and the Future of Cuba*
Explores Cuba's strained relationship with the United States, the island nation's evolving culture and politics, and prospects for U.S.–Cuba policy with the departure of Fidel Castro. $22.95, HARDCOVER.

Reese Erlich, *The Iran Agenda: The Real Story of U.S. Policy and the Middle East Crisis*
Explores the turbulent recent history between the two countries and how it has led to a showdown over nuclear technology. $14.95, PAPERBACK.

Todd Farley, *Making the Grades: My Misadventures in the Standardized Testing Industry*
Exposes the folly of many large-scale educational assessments through an alternately edifying and hilarious firsthand account of life in the testing business. $16.95, PAPERBACK.

Steven Hill, *10 Steps to Repair American Democracy*
Identifies the key problems with American democracy, especially election practices, and proposes ten specific reforms to reinvigorate it. $11.00, PAPERBACK.

Jim Hunt, *They Said What? Astonishing Quotes on American Power, Democracy, and Dissent*
Covering everything from squashing domestic dissent to stymieing equal representation, these quotes remind progressives exactly what they're up against. $12.95, PAPERBACK.

Michael Huttner and Jason Salzman, *50 Ways You Can Help Obama Change America*
Describes actions citizens can take to clean up the mess from the last administration, enact Obama's core campaign promises, and move the country forward. $12.95, PAPERBACK.

Helene Jorgensen, *Sick and Tired: How America's Health Care System Fails Its Patients*
Recounts the author's struggle to receive proper treatment for Lyme disease and examines the inefficiencies and irrationalities that she discovered in America's health care system during that five-year odyssey. $16.95, PAPERBACK.

Markos Kounalakis and Peter Laufer, *Hope Is a Tattered Flag: Voices of Reason and Change for the Post-Bush Era*
Gathers together the most listened-to politicos and pundits, activists and thinkers, to answer the question: what happens after Bush leaves office? $29.95, HARDCOVER; $16.95 PAPERBACK.

Yvonne Latty, *In Conflict: Iraq War Veterans Speak Out on Duty, Loss, and the Fight to Stay Alive*
Features the unheard voices, extraordinary experiences, and personal photographs of a broad mix of Iraq War veterans, including Congressman Patrick Murphy, Tammy Duckworth, Kelly Daugherty, and Camilo Mejia. $24.00, HARDCOVER.

Phillip Longman, *Best Care Anywhere: Why VA Health Care Is Better Than Yours,* 2nd edition
Shows how the turnaround at the long-maligned VA hospitals provides a blueprint for salvaging America's expensive but troubled health care system. $15.95, PAPERBACK.

Phillip Longman and Ray Boshara, *The Next Progressive Era*
Provides a blueprint for a re-empowered progressive movement and describes its implications for families, work, health, food, and savings. $22.95, HARDCOVER.

Marcia and Thomas Mitchell, *The Spy Who Tried to Stop a War: Katharine Gun and the Secret Plot to Sanction the Iraq Invasion*
Describes a covert operation to secure UN authorization for the Iraq war and the furor that erupted when a young British spy leaked it. $23.95, HARDCOVER.

Markos Moulitsas, *The American Taliban: How War, Sex, Sin, and Power Bind Jihadists and the Radical Right*
Highlights how American conservatives are indistinguishable from Islamic radicals except in the name of their god. $15.95, PAPERBACK.

Susan Mulcahy, ed., *Why I'm a Democrat*
Explores the values and passions that make a diverse group of Americans proud to be Democrats. $14.95, PAPERBACK.

David Neiwert, *The Eliminationists: How Hate Talk Radicalized the American Right*
Argues that the conservative movement's alliances with far-right extremists have not only pushed the movement's agenda to the right, but also have become a malignant influence increasingly reflected in political discourse. $16.95, PAPERBACK.

Christine Pelosi, *Campaign Boot Camp: Basic Training for Future Leaders*
Offers a seven-step guide for successful campaigns and causes at all levels of government. $15.95, PAPERBACK.

William Rivers Pitt, *House of Ill Repute: Reflections on War, Lies, and America's Ravaged Reputation*
Skewers the Bush Administration for its reckless invasions, warrantless wiretaps, lethally incompetent response to Hurricane Katrina, and other scandals and blunders. $16.00, PAPERBACK.

Sarah Posner, *God's Profits: Faith, Fraud, and the Republican Crusade for Values Voters*
Examines corrupt televangelists' ties to the Republican Party and unprecedented access to the Bush White House. $19.95, HARDCOVER.

Nomi Prins, *Jacked: How "Conservatives" Are Picking Your Pocket – Whether You Voted for Them or Not*
Describes how the "conservative" agenda has affected your wallet, skewed national priorities, and diminished America—but not the American spirit. $12.00, PAPERBACK.

Cliff Schecter, *The Real McCain: Why Conservatives Don't Trust Him—And Why Independents Shouldn't*
Explores the gap between the public persona of John McCain and the reality of this would-be president. $14.95, HARDCOVER.

Norman Solomon, *Made Love, Got War: Close Encounters with America's Warfare State*
Traces five decades of American militarism and the media's all-too-frequent failure to challenge it. $24.95, HARDCOVER.

John Sperling et al., *The Great Divide: Retro vs. Metro America*
Explains how and why our nation is so bitterly divided into what the authors call Retro and Metro America. $19.95, PAPERBACK.

Mark Sumner, *The Evolution of Everything: How Selection Shapes Culture, Commerce, and Nature*
Shows how Darwin's theory of evolution has been misapplied—and why a more nuanced reading of that work helps us understand a wide range of social and economic activity as well as the natural world. $15.95, PAPERBACK.

Daniel Weintraub, *Party of One: Arnold Schwarzenegger and the Rise of the Independent Voter*
Explains how Schwarzenegger found favor with independent voters, whose support has been critical to his success, and suggests that his bipartisan approach represents the future of American politics. $19.95, HARDCOVER.

Curtis White, *The Barbaric Heart: Faith, Money, and the Crisis of Nature*
Argues that the solution to the present environmental crisis may come from an unexpected quarter: the arts, religion, and the realm of the moral imagination. $16.95, PAPERBACK.

Curtis White, *The Spirit of Disobedience: Resisting the Charms of Fake Politics, Mindless Consumption, and the Culture of Total Work*
Debunks the notion that liberalism has no need for spirituality and describes a "middle way" through our red state/blue state political impasse. Includes three powerful interviews with John DeGraaf, James Howard Kunstler, and Michael Ableman. $24.00, HARDCOVER.

For more information, please visit www.p3books.com.

About This Book

This book is printed on Cascade Enviro100 Print paper. It contains 100 percent post-consumer fiber and is certified EcoLogo, Processed Chlorine Free, and FSC Recycled. For each ton used instead of virgin paper, we:

- Save the equivalent of 17 trees
- Reduce air emissions by 2,098 pounds
- Reduce solid waste by 1,081 pounds
- Reduce the water used by 10,196 gallons
- Reduce suspended particles in the water by 6.9 pounds.

This paper is manufactured using biogas energy, reducing natural gas consumption by 2,748 cubic feet per ton of paper produced.

The book's printer, Malloy Incorporated, works with paper mills that are environmentally responsible, that do not source fiber from endangered forests, and that are third-party certified. Malloy prints with soy and vegetable based inks, and over 98 percent of the solid material they discard is recycled. Their water emissions are entirely safe for disposal into their municipal sanitary sewer system, and they work with the Michigan Department of Environmental Quality to ensure that their air emissions meet all environmental standards.

The Michigan Department of Environmental Quality has recognized Malloy as a Great Printer for their compliance with environmental regulations, written environmental policy, pollution prevention efforts, and pledge to share best practices with other printers. Their county Department of Planning and Environment has designated them a Waste Knot Partner for their waste prevention and recycling programs.